CW01021658

The
with the
Tortoiseshell
Glasses

Dave Hopwood

A Few Other Books Wot Dave Has Wrote

- **Mark** – a Gospel reimagined
- **John** – a Gospel reimagined
- **Job Done** – an easy to read contemporary take on the book of Job
- **In Your Own Words** – read Dave's thoughts and add your own on some great biblical themes
- **The Bloke's Bible** – a disenchanted guy visits his local pub, reads his Bible and reflects on life
- **Raging Grace** – thoughts on life, faith and the universe
- **Top Stories** – Jesus's parables retold and unpacked
- **Film and Faith** – reflections on 66 moments from 66 films
- **The Shed** – a struggling guy takes 40 days out in a shack on a moorland monastery

Details and extracts of these and Dave's other books can be found on his website – **davehopwood.com**.

You can also sign up to receive his weekly creative writing.

© Dave Hopwood 2020

For Lynn, Amy and Lucy x

And for Liz and Martin
(thank you Martin for your help
with this and all my books)

Praise for The Boy With the Tortoiseshell Glasses –

'It's got pictures in it.'
Charles Dickens

'Thank goodness it's not as long as War & Peace.*'*
Leo Tolstoy

'It's like the phone directory. But with less romance and humour.'
Jane Austen

'It might have been more appealing if it came with some free tortoiseshell glasses.'
Samuel Pepys

'Everyone has one good book in them, I doubt it's this one.'
Aristotle

The Get-go

I heard recently that when we remember things what we're actually remembering is the last time we remembered them. So I guess the recollections in this book are all versions of what happened as I have remembered and revisited them over the years. Perhaps I have reimagined some of them. If so, I apologise. But mostly I hope you enjoy these flawed remembrances and find them helpful in some way.

I have wondered for a while about whether or not to write a kind of autobiographical book. However... there was the small matter of whether anyone would read it. After all I haven't converted a small European country, or invented a cure for hiccups, or translated the Bible into Elvish. I don't have any major triumphs to record. Things have been relatively small, and life has been fairly normal. Plus I wasn't sure if I'd already written some of these small and normal recollections in some of my other books. Apologies if I have and you've come across them before.

I enjoyed Roald Dahl's account of his early life in his book *Boy*, I liked his self-deprecating take and random memories, not trying too hard to document every bit of toast he ever ate or every trip to the restroom. I also enjoyed Matt Haig's thoughts and recollections in his book *Reasons to Stay Alive*, using various styles to record his experiences. Plus, the classic *Cup of Tea and a Sit Down* spurred me on. It's an odyssey about tea, cake and biscuits by Nicey and Wifey (yes, really.) Highly informative but full of unnecessary and entertaining meandering. So I wondered about attempting a kind of collection of musings, thoughts and misdemeanours. Hopefully not taking myself too seriously. When I do my film and faith sessions I sometimes post up this slide:

Disclaimer
The views expressed in the following hour are not necessarily the views of (whichever establishment I am in at the time). Those attending should be aware that other filmic viewpoints are available and that at times Mr. David Michael Hopwood may well be talking nonsense.

And all that rambling is merely to say I hope I don't come across too straight-faced, and sound as if I consider myself in any way grand in this bunch of ragged recollections that you now hold in your hand. Also, apologies if I come across as opinionated at times. Oh, and apologies too if you picked up this book hoping for a mention, I've been very sparing on namechecks. Plus there's no real dirt-dishing on encounters with the great and the good. Ooh, apart from once selling a theatre programme to Alvin Stardust. And I may have walked past Cliff in a department store in Woking. He was in a denim jacket I think.

So all the best with the book. Hope you get something from it and it doesn't feel too much like hard work. Maybe it will help you reflect in some way on the autobiography of your own life. And I want to say a big thankyou to all those who have befriended and encouraged me over the years.

Guess who? Still have the same hairstyle and glasses.

In A Nutshell

I may well not go into too much detail at times as I blunder clumsily through the tales in this book, so here's a kind of movie trailer of things:

- Born in Stoke on Trent 24th December 1962
- 1962-1969 cooing, crying, toddlering and early schooling in Stoke
- 1969 moved to Cornwall
- 1969-1974 Illogan Junior school
- 1974-1976 Redruth Grammar School
- 1976-1977 Redruth Comprehensive School
- 1977 moved to Weston-Super-Mare
- 1977-1979 Broadoak Comprehensive School (I see it's an Academy now)
- 1979 started work in National Westminster Bank in Oxford Street, W-S-M at the tender age of 16 (you could do that in those days)
- 1980-1981 experienced a kind of unusual 18 month conversion to Christianity
- 1981 saw a Christian mime artist, began doing Christian drama and helped start a local Youth For Christ organisation
- 1984 joined the Lee Abbey Christian community in Lynton, North Devon
- September-December 1988 left Lee Abbey and went to mime school in London
- 1989 worked freelance as a mime artist, drama writer and tutor
- 1990 formed Insight Theatre Company with four friends from Lee Abbey days

- 1992 left Insight, moved to Woking and worked solo again
- 1994 got married on the 1st September (phew! needed to remember that date correctly)
- 1996 started to fall apart
- 1997 gave up being a mime artist and drama tutor
- 1997-2001 tried to be a successful writer
- 2000 moved to a cottage in Derbyshire, still trying to be a writer, still falling apart
- 2001 returned to Lee Abbey for short bursts as summer then autumn workers
- 2002 returned to Lee Abbey as full-time community members
- 2002 Amy, our first daughter, was born in March
- 2002 I read a book called *Praying the Movies*, it was the beginning of something
- 2002-2011 wrote and directed summer, winter and Easter shows at Lee Abbey, started speaking and drawing on all kinds of contemporary media
- 2004-2005 wrote *The Bloke's Bible*
- 2011 left Lee Abbey and started working as a Christian writer and speaker
- 2013 Lucy, our second daughter, was born in July
- 2020 wrote this book

That was a hefty nutshell really, but it's there in case you need a timeline of sorts. I may well be a tad random in the pages that follow.

Some things I recall liking when I was at school

- Jaws (the book)
- Jaws (the film)
- Recording songs off the radio
- Writing stories
- *The Mystery of the Green Dragon,* an interactive adventure book
- Making up whodunit plays and acting them out with friends in my best mate's back garden
- Watching the *Whodunit* series on TV
- Watching the *Colditz* series on TV
- Playing *Best man dead* – in which you murdered all your friends with a gun/grenade/flamethrower and then chose the one who had died the most spectacularly
- *The Magic Roundabout* and *Tom and Jerry* in that five minute slot before the news came on
- Tintin (on TV)
- Tintin (the books)
- School summer holidays (seven weeks! Felt like forever)
- My 88 boots (think *All Stars* nowadays)
- Playing *English and Germans*
- Unexpectedly scoring a try in a rugby lesson
- Redruth Grammar School
- The book *The Otterbury Incident*
- The book *Run Baby Run*
- Girls (although they were scary too)

- Queen, The Drifters, The Beach Boys and Abba (in other words the first cassette albums I bought and played to death)
- Radio 1 (Tony Blackburn, 'Diddy' David Hamilton, Johnny Walker)
- The films *The Magnificent Seven, The Great Escape, The Longest Day* and *Whistle Down the Wind*
- *The Three Investigators* series of books
- Enid Blyton's book *The Six Bad Boys*
- *The Banana Splits* TV show
- The Sunday TV series *Alias Smith and Jones*
- The Sunday TV Series *The Last of the Mohicans*
- Basil Brush ('Dirty Gerty from number 30! Boom boom!')
- My plastic Disney projector, hand cranked, my first endeavours as a projectionist, I now work once a week as a real one
- Disney time on bank holiday Mondays
- *Papillon*, the film, I didn't read the book till much later, love both though
- *Pink Panther* movies, fell about laughing with my dad
- Steve McQueen's outfit in *The Great Escape*, I'm fairly sure at some point I began wearing similar white jeans and purple t-shirt (along with my 88 boots)
- The song *Sugar Sugar* by the animated group *The Archies*
- Elton John and Kiki Dee - *Don't go breaking my heart*

- *The Legend of Xanadu* by Dave Dee, Dozy, Beaky, Mick and Tich, the first single I ever bought
- The song *Imagine*, though the more popular it has become the less I've been grabbed by it
- *Charade*, with Cary Grant and Audrey Hepburn, brilliant, funny, thrilling and mysterious
- *Incident at Owl Creek Bridge*, we were shown this short film in an English lesson and I'll be forever grateful. Made me fall in love with twisty-turny stories that trick you. It's on YouTube
- Duelling with my friend next door, flicking real burning matches at one another (don't try this at home)
- The poster of Clint Eastwood on my wardrobe door, looking all Spaghetti Western-like, torn out of the *Radio Times* I believe
- The day I left school at 16
- Bugsy Malone

Bugsy Malone features the great opening line about a character called Roxy Robinson – 'if it was raining brains, Roxy wouldn't even get wet'. For me it's one of the great openers, ranking alongside the first line of Peter Benchley's *Jaws* – 'the great fish moved silently through the dark water'. (Let's face it – it could be an alternative start to Jonah.)

Just this morning, reading a newspaper article, I came across something I'd completely forgotten. I loved Alan Parker's *Bugsy Malone*. The book of the film, that is. This was the extraordinary thing. I didn't see the film till years later, I don't even know when I did see it, but around the time it came out (1976) someone bought me a copy of the book, complete with stills from the movie, and something about this mythical, custard pie spattered tale was irresistible.

For years I only ever saw the stills in the book, but so much about Bugsy really grabbed me, the kid in the middle, the lone hero coming to the rescue, the edgy nice guy, out on his own, willing to take chances to save the day. Plus it's a tale told in that sassy, film noir kind of way, in the vernacular of mobsters, speakeasies and Tommy guns, conjuring those otherworldly images of streetwise kids in a land of pay-offs and hoodlums. I felt I was loitering on the edge of a whole other universe, so thrilling and dangerous and engrossing. A place peopled by the likes of Roxy, Ritzy, Blousy, Bugsy, Snake Eyes, Fat Sam, Knuckles, Tallulah and Dandy Dan.

Am I overegging this? Perhaps. I probably perceive more in it now than I did back then. I just know that Bugsy, the cool maverick good guy in that smooth-talking gangster paradise, really appealed to me. Years later I wrote a parable about fears, featuring two hoodlums called Moxy and Sloot; and then later again I wrote *Spondulix*, a longer yarn about the lure of cash, set in a timeless gangster-laden city. I wonder now if both were subconsciously inspired by my forgotten love for the tale of Bugsy Malone.

Things I recall not liking much when I was at school

- Games and P.E. lessons (apart from the moment when I astonishingly scored a try in rugby)
- The day we were going to 'go comprehensive' and for months the word on the street (or in the playground) was that we were all going to get beaten up by all the kids from the secondary school we were joining
- Trips to the dentist
- School after we went comprehensive
- Radio 2
- Matt Monro (found his songs depressing) sorry if you're a fan
- My face turning red when I had to answer questions in class
- My face turning red in general when I was embarrassed (still not a fan now)
- Trips to the outside toilet in my gran's house
- Summer holidays coming to an end and thinking of the things I could have done with those seven weeks

Stokey

I was born in Stoke on Trent, on 24th December [h] 1962. It was cold and snowy. So much so that my mum had a fire in her bedroom. I don't mean burning the furniture or anything. My parents, I believe, had an open fireplace in those days in their bedroom. So my first gurgles took place to the sound of crackling wood and hissing coal. In the heart of the Potteries. And this means I am technically a *Stokey* though I have long since lost most of the accent. It's still a 'bath' though and not a 'baarrth', for goodness sake. ☺

Me and my sister Liz. We haven't changed a bit.

Trains, Bikes and Lavatories

My grandparents on my mum's side had an outside toilet and no fridge. (In the outside toilet or the house). So nipping to the loo of an evening meant a trek down the garden in the dark. I remember the warm cosy smell of toast under the gas grill at their house, and Saturday wrestling on the telly. Granddad's pipe and penknife and his tobacco tin kept handy on a shelf in the cupboard with the sliding door beside his chair, over by the window. The grey cardigan he always wore with the little pockets in. He had a quiet dignity and was very tall. Though I was very small when I knew him. Gran was shorter and busier and chattier. It was she who made the warm and cosy toast.

I never met my dad's dad, he died before I was born, but I remember his mum, my grandma. Dad and I played cards at her home sometimes so my auntie Olive, who lived with Grandma, could go to church. On one visit her house was jammed with cousins and their families. No idea what the occasion was but I remember crowding around the telly to watch *Land of the Giants*. My dad worked in Minton China, as a factory foreman I think. So many of our wider family did, uncles and aunts. I heard stories of my aunt hand-painting the gold onto new cups. My dad started working there as a teenager, but when the chance came to move to a job in Cornwall he took it.

He worked for a yarn factory at first, but when that closed he became a Ministry of Defence policeman.

I only have a few memories of life in Stoke, we moved to Cornwall when I was six and that seems to be around the time my little grey cells went into hyperdrive, and my ability to retain information kicked in proper. I do remember however, one Christmas Eve night in Stoke (I think I was about four) hearing footsteps on the stairs and being convinced it was the sound of Santa's snow-covered boots as he dragged his huge and bursting sack up to my room. Even as I write this now I'm still convinced it was the sleigh rider really. All decked up in his bleached hipster beard and his big red maternity trousers. I mean, who else could it have possibly been in the deep dark hours of the night before Christmas?

I also recall having a large train set fixed to a board the size of my bed. I laid it out on top of my bed at least once (maybe lots of times), with the train travelling on it, whilst I lay underneath the bed studying the dust and listening to the train chugging around and around. There was something cosy and pleasing about the sound. The train set sadly didn't make the move to Cornwall. Most likely went to another good Stokey home.

Another early memory is of having Lucozade when I was ill. Maybe in bed, maybe not. Oh and that's just reminded me. I also recall trying to sleep on the sofa one night having had an upset stomach, and waking up just in time to throw up in a bucket. My dad was nearby and no doubt doing his best to make me feel better. I doubt if I was sipping Lucozade that night. I don't think that had much to do with Christmas, but I was often feeling a bit on the dodgy side by the time Christmas was done and dusted, too much excitement with a birthday and a nativity to celebrate all in two days.

Bike riding! I have a picture in my head of my dad holding on to the saddle of my wee bike when he was teaching me to travel sans stabilisers. I struggled to get it and practically gave up. Then suddenly – maybe when I wasn't trying too hard – a moment of joy as I discovered I could do it! Sometimes the way, isn't it.

We were living in Oakhill Avenue when a huge van pitched up to take us away. It was a consensual arrangement. My parents had paid for the thing so we could move to Cornwall. I was six and I vaguely recall looking out of my parents' bedroom window in wonder at the size of this lorry. Everything was about to change. Our address, my school, the weather (apparently it was always warm in Cornwall), the decade and the price of everything. It was 1969. Sun, sand and the seventies here we come. Along with decimalisation.

The Seventies

- Snake belts
- Chopper bikes
- Chunky flip-flops
- Space hoppers
- The Bay City Rollers
- *Killer Queen*
- *Bohemian Rhapsody* on Top of the Pops
- Bone handled sheath knives
- *Ernie and his milk cart*
- The Osmonds
- David Cassidy on my sister's wall (a poster, not the man himself stapled up there)
- Performing *King of the Swingers* from *The Jungle Book* at school (ever the performer)
- Crackerjack
- *Disney Time* on bank holiday Mondays
- The Beach Boys' 20 Golden Greats
- The Pillsbury Doughboy
- Feather cuts
- The Michelin Man
- The Wombles
- Cowboy films
- War films
- Black and white tellies
- Matching shirts and ties (And here's the proof –)

Quicksand

We moved to a village called Illogan (pronounced Luggan by the locals) and the rest is history. Actually, the rest is my early school years. I walked then biked to junior school in the village. Till I was old enough for the eleven-plus to transport me to Redruth Grammar. When we first arrived in Cornwall we had no car or telephone. Try telling that to the kids of today and they won't believe you. We didn't live in an 'ole in the ground, but we did have to move into temporary accommodation while we waited for our bungalow to be built. ('There were four of us living in't shoe box in't middle o't road.')

One evening as I trudged up the unfinished road past our new house, the ground became so muddy that my wellies got stuck fast. I imagined myself sinking and being swallowed whole, like one of those cowboys in quicksand in the films I loved. Terrified I left my wellies protruding from the mire and ran home sobbing. Ah… happy days.

Sometimes, early on a Saturday morning, I would sneak into the kitchen with a Mars Bar (they were bigger and thicker back then) and slice it into thin slivers to take back to bed and savour whilst reading Jim Starling books and Lemon Kelly novels. Boys Own adventures featuring characters with names like Goggles and Nip. And of course there were

Richmal Crompton's *Just William* books, hardback tomes from the library. Big and scuffed and stuffed full of thick pages bearing the occasional interesting stain. I recently read that starting a new book is like going on a train ride, well these tales of derring-do were certainly my epic journeys back then. I longed to create my own and for my first attempt came up with *Basil the Friendly Ghost* about a boy called Barney who discovers a friendly ghost in his house, called, you guessed it, Basil. I'd been reading Clive King's *Stig of the Dump* and think I nicked the name Barney from that classic. I think I wrote a sequel called *The Inch and a Half High Robot* about Barney, Basil and Bolts – the inch and a half high robot. My dad rediscovered them for me a few decades ago, but sadly somehow I managed to lose them again.

The other great read was C. Day Lewis's *The Otterbury Incident*. How I loved, and still love that book. Two gangs of post-war boys on an adventure to capture some local thugs. Thrilling and wonderful stuff. First read to us by Mr Tuck, who later got me to read my stories to the class. They weren't that great, but having a teacher who believes in you is dynamite. More of that later.

Terror

It was whilst reading one of Richmal Crompton's books, on a Mars-sliver-savouring Saturday morning that I came across a chapter entitled *William and the Blue Satan*. I remember feeling a little nervous about the dark nature of this episode. I steeled myself and trekked on through the first few pages. Nothing. No sign of anything dark or scary at all. Just a tale of bumbling William and a bit of cloth. Oh! Right! Of course. I see! *William and the Blue **Satin***! I still feel a little foolish at the thought of my inability to read that title properly. In too much of a hurry probably. Still am. I continue to be rubbish at reading instructions. That said, I was a sensitive child and cautious of anything scary. Though oddly, I was also fascinated by stories about big old haunted houses. The Scooby Doo annual was a must-read!

I only read *The Three Investigators and the Secret of Terror Castle* because we had some reading time in class and I had forgotten a book, so I looked over the shoulder of a friend who was currently ploughing his way though the spooky tale. It felt somehow dangerous and a little heady to be venturing into a book with terror in the title about which I knew nothing. How terrible was this castle going to be? Was I *allowed* to read a book of this kind? Turned out to be spooky in a very addictive kind of way, from them on I couldn't put the Three Investigators down. I was hooked on their spine-tingling mysteries.

We Really Shouldn't Have Survived

We lived in a quiet circular close of bungalows, and I soon befriended, and did my best to boss around, a gaggle of friends. We used to play games in the street, British Bulldog, stuck in the mud, tig, and when we weren't doing that we'd stage whodunnit plays in the back gardens for our bemused parents. We'd kick a ball in the road and zoom about on our bikes. We'd form teams to hunt, chase or murder each other, and I'd frequently hide under that big oil tank in our back garden, with the damp soil smell and the weeds and the bugs and the darkness. I remember drinking water out of plant pots and not feeling too chipper afterwards, and picking raw beans and peas that my parents were growing on bamboo canes, then eating them for a kind of picnic. Come to think of it our garage held a steady supply of bamboo canes, they came in handy for us as makeshift weapons of course, spears and swords.

We used to clamber over a nearby wall into a wooded area we nicknamed 'bush' and drape our bodies over the thick winding branches there. I wasn't particularly outdoorsy or sporty, but when I look at my own children and the ways of the world now I sometimes wonder if ours wasn't the last generation for whom the great outdoors was so great. But then perhaps every generation thinks that.

I'm sure there are still lots of kids who continue to love playing outside, but for us the indoor options were limited. We had train sets and Scalextric sets and of course the telly. But as far as any onscreen pastimes went, the basic and pedestrian computer game of Pong was only just starting to sneak across our TV screens. And it was my neighbour who had one of those. Not me. I had a chemistry set and a *Colditz* game and shoeboxes full of cars and plastic *Airfix* soldiers. Which we often took outside and set in crevices in the garden rockery. Even as our parents were out there tidying the garden we were messing it up again. Later, as a teenager, a friend and I took pot shots at the larger soldiers with my air rifle. Crack! Ping! 'Oi!' from my dad as a ricocheting pellet sailed past his ear. Simpler times.

There were times when I did withdraw from the scrambling and scurrying and pretending to kill each other. I'd hide away and make attempts at writing stories in precious hardbacked notebooks of various colours and sizes, spidery writing done with my *Papermate* biro or school fountain pen. I started

many tales over the years which I never finished. I rather like this old cover with its nod to *Jaws* – *Gums*.

God or the devil?

It was the middle of a sermon. I was sitting in the choir at Illogan church in Cornwall, looking at a bit of paper which had fluttered off the choir stall opposite and was lying there, glaring up at me like a bad stain on the carpet, wondering whether I should pick it up. Feeling like I really *should* pick it up, but not sure whether it was God or the devil urging me to do so. I sat through the entire sermon wondering about this and, I think, I may well have eventually picked up the piece of paper. But I'm not sure. It was a long time ago, in the early 1970s, and to this day I'm unsure who or what was urging me on. Though I hopefully feel it matters less now than it did then. At the time I probably did all kinds of mental gymnastics over this vital thing, ending up in quite a stew. To mix my metaphors for a moment. Needless to say I can't remember a single word of the sermon.

Stress over the smallest things continues to play in the background of my life. Like a kind of white noise. I worry about sitting in the right place in public. And whether the seat I eventually sit on is clean enough. I worry about what comes out of the back end of a dog and whether I will step in any of it when I'm out and about. A reasonable concern you might say, but when it stops you actually going for a walk down certain country lanes... I worry about putting the right socks on in the morning. I worry that I might upset folks by saying the wrong thing. I worry about upsetting God in the same way. I worry about locking the door and if the tap is dripping.

I have worried about so many things over the years (there is a list later on), most of them too mad to mention out loud. But I have come to realise that the madness is often a shadow side of so many good things in my life. For one thing I have a very active imagination. And one of the results of that is one day having the idea for the book you are now holding called *The Boy With the Tortoiseshell Glasses.* So... you know... and also, to reference a bit of Bible for a moment, when we're honest about our madness, troubles and weaknesses, we can help others with the help we have found from God.

Rev Counta

There is a Christian song by a guy called Ishmael with the first line – 'Father God I wonder how I managed to exist without the knowledge of your parenthood and your loving care…' (and breathe) I first encountered Ishmael in the guise of Rev Counta and the Speedoze on an album of fast paced three-minute Ska songs. More my sort of thing back then really. But I mention the other song because, well, I can't really sing it. Nothing to do with having to reach any high notes. (For that sort of snag try singing *His name is higher than any other* in the wrong key – now that will get your vocal cords screaming for relief.)

But I mention Ishmael's song with the lyrics in mind. I can't recall a time when I wondered about how I was going to ever exist without heavenly parental knowledge. 'Cause I'm dead fortunate. Really fortunate. I grew up in a Christian family and had the knowledge downloaded in my DNA. Admittedly our family faith was to do a lot of maturing over the years, but we went to church, and said grace at meals, and always collectively believed in the God of the Bible. And for that, I am well grateful.

Goggles

I don't ever remember being nicknamed or insulted or in any way tagged with the name *Goggles* though I have worn glasses since my early years. I did feel burdened by them (this was long before the '90s girl band *All Saints* made spectacle wearing cool and sexy) and as soon as I had enough money in my pocket to buy a pair of gas permeable contact lenses I was down the opticians quicker than you can say 'but-John-Lennon-looks-okay'. These days tortoise-shell glasses hold a certain retro appeal. But back then I felt specky and four-eyed. I felt it made me look unsporty. Which to be honest I was – glasses or no glasses.

I was also shy at school, and I found certain things highly embarrassing. Things like, well – girls really. Oh and having to answer questions in front of the rest of the class. I was fairly intelligent, and regularly featured in the top three when we had end-of-term exams. But my one and only desire was to escape the educational environment. Then I'd never have to be embarrassed playing – or not able to play – sports. Hopefully at some point I'd turn into *Mr Cool* and have no problems with girls.

A week after leaving school I started working in NatWest bank, and for the first few months I tried not wearing glasses as I hadn't worn them when I first dropped in to look around, and I felt too self-conscious to suddenly turn up in them. For a while I was living the dream, life without specs, which was fine just so long as no one asked me what time it was on the clock on the far wall. It was around this time that I went looking for the nearest set of gas permeables. I guess I have always had this thing about needing to look presentable in a certain way, to look 'right'. Even though no one else may notice or care. I was terrified of sticking out, getting it wrong, looking foolish. Still am sometimes. The embarrassment threshold is jolly low.

Whippersnappers

We were lining up to go into class at junior school, I was about seven I think. It was the usual kind of thing, a bunch of small dishevelled bodies squished together in a ragged straggle of a queue against a huge stone wall. As we stood there I recall seeing some tearaway from my year, or perhaps the year above, doing something naughty and daring. Goodness knows what now. Obviously something really dangerous, like pinching someone, or running around the yard in a highly illegal fashion.

The thing I remember though is my unexpressed urge to encourage him on, as if I wanted to be seen as a part of his derring-do. A brother in his rebellion. 'Well done mate!' I might have called as the teacher dragged him away. 'Go for it! Cool! Wicked!' Except that we didn't say things like 'Go for it', or 'Wicked' back then. And even 'Cool' was a word that seemed to belong to a previous outdated decade at that point. But it's an odd memory isn't it. And it shows what daft things stay with us. I can't remember so many vital moments, or even what day it is sometimes, but I can recall watching a rebel kid running riot in the playground. And wanting somehow to encourage him on. To be a part of his cheekiness.

I still warm to rebels. That's one of the reasons I continue to love punk rock. I once heard a BBC producer describe Johnny Rotten as the kind of boy you wouldn't ask to give out the scissors in class. Too unruly, too reckless. Unpredictable.

I think that's why I love the biblical prophets. Let's face it they may well have been the kind of whippersnappers who ran round the schoolyard when they should have been standing in line. You wouldn't invite Isaiah to a party would you? He might come naked. Highly embarrassing, unless it was that kind of party. And Jeremiah was a bit of a killjoy if ever there was one. Ezekiel might grab the cheese and pineapple on sticks and start building a predictive model of your town in ruins. Or he might scatter the celery sticks across the carpet and tell them to live again. I love them for all of that. They were boat rockers, cage rattlers, trend buckers. Not for their own good, but for the good of those taking note.

I wish I could be more like them. I want to be different. Even though the thought of doing such reckless things scares the socks off me. Perhaps that's why I was willing to do street theatre, standing out in the rain with a startlingly white face, grabbing folks attention, making them take a second look. And maybe that's why I'm attempting to write a different kind of 'Christian' book. One where wayward seven year olds and aging punk rockers get to hold the stage, even for a short while.

You Got a Friend

I used to think that the chorus of James Taylor's classic song went like this – *Winter, spring, summer will fall…* Mainly because I was only about seven or eight when another boy, he may have been called Mark, sang it to me repeatedly in the playground, ending with the line he hoped would make an impact – *'You got a friend.'* Because of course, that's exactly what he wanted to be – my friend. Back then I had no idea that to our chums across the water Autumn was not Autumn at all – no, it was Fall. So Mr Taylor actually wrote and sang – *Winter, spring summer **or** fall…* Whether the boy probably known as Mark knew about the whole Autumn/Fall controversy I do not know, but he sang it to me again and again, and it may well have been the first time I ever heard it.

The other night I watched the concert movie *Amazing Grace* in which Aretha Franklin sings a gospel version of that song. The concert took place in a church back in 1972, and it reminded me of my friend, and I realised that Aretha may well have been singing her version at the time that the boy probably known as Mark was singing his. Who knew? Aretha's version also played with the wording. Her version was all about another kind of friendship, the friendship we find in Jesus. It was the highlight of the movie for me as the gospel choir and all those attending threw themselves wholeheartedly into the celebration of friendship with God.

In recent times I have come to love the fact that Jesus said that we were no longer servants, but his friends. Radical of course. How many gods ever had humans for friends? Eh? None, that's how many, until Jesus pitched up making folks laugh, cry, hope, dream and change the world. One smile at a time.

The whole subject of friends turned out to be a tricky area for me. I'm grateful for the many friends I have made over the years, but it turns out that – like Ancient Hebrew, Elvish, Klingon, DIY and knitting – it's yet another subject I'm just not very good at. I've turned out to be quite a private person (I'm in good company, David Bowie, Denzel Washington, Robert DeNiro, JD Salinger, Sandra Bullock, Gretta Garbo, John the Baptist – they are/were all pretty private people).

Okay. Maybe I lied about John the B. He was fairly out there. But he had little choice, he had to live his life in public. He might secretly have been more than happy to sit at home, listening to Simeon Wood, reading Adrian Plass, curled up in his slippers and munching on Doritos. By the way, listening to Simeon Wood is highly recommendable, whether you're a publicly private or privately public person. Me? I'm off the scale private. A raging introvert. So I make friends as much as I can. But I'm happiest sitting at home, listening to (I kid you not) *Bat Out of Hell* by Simeon Wood, reading Adrian Plass, curled up in my slippers and munching on Doritos.

No One Forgets a Good Teacher

There is an old advert in which famous people appear on screen and mention other people you've never heard of. The advert closes with the strapline: 'No one forgets a good teacher.'

One abiding and dearly-loved memory of my time in Illogan Junior School is of Mr Tuck reading us *The Otterbury Incident*. He was our teacher in the second year and he read us this classic tale of derring-do in instalments, at the end of school each day. I was so captivated by the story that when I missed the last episode due to illness (probably a cold, I think I had a lot of them) I borrowed the revered paperback from Mr Tuck and was allowed to take it home and read the denouement for myself. Wow! I was allowed to borrow Mr Tuck's book! And what a story! I can still remember holding that well-worn copy in my hands. With that brilliant orange and yellow sketch on the cover of the battle in Skinner's yard. It's by C. Day Lewis, Daniel's dad.

Many years later I swallowed my pride and shuffled into a bookshop in High Wycombe and discovered to my delight that it was still available. So I now have my own copy! Oh wonder of wonders! It's in serious danger of being my all-time favourite book. The memories are still so vivid, so precious, of an adventure that was so wondrous, so clever, so daring and thrilling back then.

I began writing my own stories around this time and it was good old Mr Tuck who invited me to read at least one of them to the class. It wasn't great and full of glaring mistakes but his desire to encourage me was so precious and important to me. Years later, at 34, on one of my pilgrimages back to Illogan, my wife and I stumbled across a relatively new headstone in the local graveyard. I was genuinely shocked to find it was Mr Tuck, my wonderful teacher, who had once seemed immortal, yet was now here, having died at 59.

The story I read to the class had been inspired by one of my first cinema trips. My dad took me to see a re-release of *The Longest Day*, one of his favourites, and I got all inspired to write my own tale of two fictional brothers going to fight on that fateful day.

The first film I went to see was probably *101 Dalmatians*, but the more vivid early cinema memory is of going to see the wonderful *Whistle Down the Wind* starring Hayley Mills. I fell in love with her and the film that day. And am still a little bit in love with both of them. I realise now that *Whistle Down the Wind* is a revisiting of the story of Jesus, something that passed me by back then. However, maybe, just maybe, it planted a creative seed in my subconscious, a desire to retell the Bible tales. Or perhaps I'm just overthinking it. I tend to do that.

Dybbing

At some point in the early seventies my dad did an amazing thing. He started a cub pack in our village. From scratch! Having never done anything like it before. And for a whole generation of lads he offered a chance to learn knots, wear a uniform, go camping and generally have a heck of a good time together. We dybbed and dobbed, earned badges and discovered names like Akela. You see our pack wasn't your run of the mill Scouting Association pack, oh no. We were Baden Powell cubs. Looking different. Being different. Harking back to the roots of Kipling and his Jungle Book tales.

We wore our white neckerchiefs with pride. Though they may not have stayed white for too long. We toured the neighbourhood on Saturday mornings collecting newspapers for recycling. We held jumble sales to raise money. We messed about in the woods and on the beach. Played wide games and sang Ging Gang Goolie round the fire. We rambled, physically and verbally. We had our own special wolf ear salutes. Two fingers held in a v shape beside your head. But not facing the rude way. Along with my mates I was a sixer, heading up a line of younger cubs. We were kings.

And all went well until we got too old. Then we needed a scout troop. So the leaders started one. And I was all at sea. I couldn't cope with all the physical stuff, the great outdoors life, perhaps an early indication of what was to come. I live in my head, and the rigours of teenage scouting left me floundering. I didn't know what was going on at the time. I guess I felt a failure. I'm not a quick learner and struggled with the new skills. I felt weak and exposed. I just couldn't fit in. I panicked. So my dad helped out, he made me an assistant at the cub pack.

And I'll always be grateful. Perhaps there was something there too about struggling to be a team player. I did better if I could be part of leading others. Blending in and conforming? Hmm. Not so much.

Doo-Dee-Doo-Doo...

I used to catch the bus to the grammar school each morning from a crossroads in our village of Illogan. When I say *our* village, we didn't own it, my dad wasn't lord of the manor or anything. A few of us grammar school types used to hang around in a fairly grumpy straggle. On certain days one lad, a boy in the year above me, used to stand there quietly singing, 'Doo dee doo doo doo, dee doo, dee doo, doo doo...' You'll no doubt recognise the tune from my rendition there... No? Really?? You can't tell from a few doo dee doos like that??? You do surprise me.

Anyway, it's the start of *Singing in the Rain*. And my bus queue friend used to sing it to himself on days when he had games or P.E. because he figured that if he sang about the possibility of singing in the rain, there might well be a possibility of not doing sports in the rain. I knew how he felt. I longed for a downpour at times. There were so many sports and so many ways that I could get them wrong. Football, rugby, basketball, athletics, cross-country running ... and no doubt many more. It was terrifying. And deeply embarrassing. The fear of looking stupid, the fear of getting it wrong. The fear of being exposed as the clumsy twerp who couldn't kick a ball straight. The fear of being left on that touchline not being picked... till there was no one else left to pick.

Plus there was the fear of being beaten to a pulp, identifiable only by dental records or acne traces, as we passed through the secondary school territory to reach the secondary school sports hall. Because our ancient grammar school didn't have one of its own. As far as I know very little violence ever took place on those Monday after-lunch treks. But fear lurked at my door every Monday morning as I anticipated that appalling venturing. Oh the joy of leaving school at 16 and not having to do compulsory sports anymore. In the evening after my last day I felt relieved and elated that it was all over… as I stood near the darkest edge of a local recreation ground, avoiding taking part in a youth club game of rounders. Who'd have expected that! Left school, and immediately discovered I would still occasionally have the need to dodge physical activity.

Another tune that got sung to me in the grammar school days was the theme from *The Ellery Queen Whodunnit*. (Best to YouTube it.) A new friend Jonathan and a couple of his mates used to sing it to me 'cause they knew I loved this mystery series. It wasn't out of spite though, not at all. Jonathan and I became really close friends, and eventually ended up being best men to each other. He's the one person from Redruth Grammar that I still have some contact with. We shared the same zany sense of humour, a disdain for games lessons, a love of stories and *The Ellery Queen* theme tune.

When I attempted my first novel – *Who-the-hell-dunnit* – a dark and comical tale of our teachers at RGS being bumped off in appropriate fashion (the chemistry master dying of poisonous fumes in the chemical cupboard, that sort of thing) Jonathan was my advisor in chief, helping me to concoct the various murderous scenarios.

Later he would instil a love of all things 007 in me when he lent me his copy of the Fleming novel *On Her Majesty's Secret Service*. We would go on to watch a whole stack of Bond movies over the years. He was a big fan of the music and introduced me to John Barry. When I say *introduced* I don't mean they were great buddies, or that he was holding him captive in the attic or anything of that ilk. After I left Cornwall we kept in touch, sending each other cassettes with our latest news on, and staying in each other's homes from time to time. He later moved to Norwich, while I moved here, there and everywhere. His was a friendly and welcome bolthole when my time in *Insight* occasionally got intense, but I'm getting ahead of myself…

Bogs

Redruth Grammar school had extraordinary bogs. Sorry, toilets. (We knew them as the bogs.) The things were housed in an ancient stone-walled edifice in the schoolyard. It was dark, dank and dingy with a very low ceiling, and I think I only ever ventured in there once. It was the sort of place you might discover the skeleton of some old villain from the 1700s, still chained to the wall next to the urinals. Which I think were also still there from the 1700s. And of course there was the smell.

But oddly what I recall most, is some graffiti etched on to the damp plaster. *No matter how much you shake your peg the drops always fall down your leg.* I was horrified and fascinated by this curious saying. And as you can see, it has stayed with me down the decades. Perhaps it's something to do with the writer in me. Just couldn't forget that bit of lavatorial poetry. After all, it's creative rather than rude, and it rhymes. Not something you can say of most toilet trivia. More recently I spotted this scribbled line in a motorway service station loo. *Alens exist.* To which someone had replied: *So do spelling lessons.* ☺

The caretaker most likely breathed his last in those school bogs (though I think we all nearly did that) in a suitably gruesome fashion in *Who-the-hell-dunnit.* I think he may have been the first to go. If you see what I mean.

Brothel Creepers and Liquorice Legs

Now you must realise – we're talking about the 1970s here. As mentioned earlier, I turned seven at the end of 1969 so much of my schooling took place in that glorious, cheesy, wide-trousered decade. By the time I made it to Redruth Grammar school in 1974 kipper ties and liquorice legs were all the rage. We used to wear our mile wide school ties as short as possible, they were barely more than cravats really. And those liquorice legs? Well, they were those dayglo ankle socks that bore a striking resemblance to the striped black and yellow/green/pink Liquorice Allsorts. We also wore 'bags' – that is – trousers that were wider than the Grand Canyon, sporting pockets on the ample legs and waistbands with a dozen buttons. Took forever to do the things up. But we wore them with pride.

Along with our hefty crepe-soled brothel creepers. As far I know no one in my form, 1G then 2G, ever crept around brothels in them. But we loved 'em. And the heftier the sole the better. We looked cooler than Showaddywaddy. Which brings me nicely to the music. Bowie was on the rise, after shedding his Ziggy Stardust skin, Glam was on the wane, Queen were rhapsodically bohemian and Showaddywaddy went strolling up Buddy Holly's *Three steps to heaven*. What none of us could foresee was the explosion in a safety pin factory heading our way. Yep. Punk.

Happy Anarchy

Redruth Grammar was small by later school experiences. Only 600 pupils. Not all my friends had good times there but for me the two years I spent at that school were by far the happiest. I felt a part of something in a way that was difficult in the larger, sprawling comprehensive schools I attended later. Our form, 1G then 2G, used to band together at lunch- times and play a mad version of British Bulldog, hurling ourselves at one another, as we looped around the outside of the large main building complex. We bantered about music, TV programmes and bodily functions, and had nicknames for each other and the teachers.

For a while we all became 'Fat'. Fat Hop, Fat Ham, Fat Chess, Fat Bes. You get the idea. Nothing to do with our size it just was. Maybe it was all Fat Sam's fault, now I think of it, you know with Bugsy Malone gracing the silver screen. Our teachers were known by old-fashioned names like *Taffy* and *Alfie*. To us anyway. They wore black gowns from a bygone era and expected us to stand up straight and take our hands out of our pockets when speaking to them. We had bulky helmet shaped haircuts, that gradually morphed into various styles which we perceived as trendy. Not me though. I stuck with the helmet look for a good few years. Those halcyon days were doomed though. We lived in trepidation of September 1976, when the Grammar School would keel over and the comprehensive system would kick in. Everything would change.

Needless to say we didn't all die on the first day back, there was more chaos than carnage. But there was no bloodbath just a muddle of lessons. Our class of 2G was hacked unceremoniously in half, something I've never really recovered from, 50% of the class going into one stream, the other 50% into another. And that I always say, is when I began to lose interest in education. Then we started to hear about a little known band called The Sex Pistols. I was horrified. It all sounded dreadfully noisy and dangerous. Not half as melodic as Showaddywaddy's *Under the Moon of Love* or ELO's *Living Thing* for goodness sake. But punk was here to stay and though I was two years late to that particularly snarly party, I would get there. And never quite be the same.

In the meantime I was only at Redruth Comp for a year. By the Summer of '77, while the big news on the street was about the sad death of Elvis, the news in our house was about moving to Yeovil. Then no, change of plan, to Weston-Super-Mare. All to do with my dad's job in the MOD police. I skived my last day at school as there was talk (again) of being beaten to a pulp. Just me this time. My 'mates' wanted to give me a send-off. Thanks fellas. I stayed home. And we up-sticked again. But not before, at some point, I took part in sport's day. I was for the high jump. Yea, really.

The Joy of Losers

To this day I think I should have won. Well, come second anyway. Somehow I found myself for the high jump. Or rather in the high jump. Sports day 197-something. There's clearly been a mistake because here I am competing in the finals. Trying to jump that bar. I got down to the final four, and then three of us ended up second. Oh well, a shared silver. I'll take that. Or rather – no I won't. Because 'apparently' when the result was broken down I had made more attempts at the jumps than the others. So not even a bronze for me. Not even a chocolate button. I failed. Somehow, even though three of us could jump an equal height, one of us jumped a less equal height then the others. Me. ME!!! So-o-o-o-o disappointed. I mean, so-o-o-o-o-o-o-o-o-o-o-o-o-o-o disappointed. My one chance at Olympic glory and yet... nothing. Of course it doesn't still hurt. Not at all. No way. You can quite clearly see that!!! 😊

Failure is not fun. Triumph is fun. Winning is a blast. Being carried shoulder high, girls fainting at your feet, medals clanking around your neck. That's fun. Losing. Not so much. And yet... and yet... what do we find Jesus saying, on a hot day in Galilee, surrounded by also-rans. A whole bunch of folks who came fourth in life's high jump. Blessed are those who crash and burn because they will know a very kind of success. Drat! You mean I can't be one of those have-it-all celebrities with a quadrillion

Twitter followers and shiny merchandise that shouts about my successful life? Ohhh. It's not fair.

Luke loves the underdogs. And as a result I like Luke. I love his tales of tax collectors and widows and prostitutes. Folks whose hearts might well have leapt when they heard the new rabbi in town say, 'God is with the poor, the grieving, the lost.' I wanted God to test me with fame and riches but it looks very much as if he won't play my games. He'd rather meet me in that old potholed place called reality. Where everybody lives really. Even if you have a quadrillion Twitter followers.

I think there is a lot of truth in old Mr Kipling's saying. Not the one about his exceedingly good cakes, but the other one. About meeting triumph and disaster and treating both imposters the same. I'm trying to learn that. That my value rating is not in how much I fail or succeed, or how many Twitter followers I have. But in Him. In His appreciation of me. And my appreciation of Him. The one who thought of high jumping, poems and the stuff that goes into those exceedingly good cakes.

Diamonds A...in't That Great

Despite being an avid movie watcher I'm not always that quick on the uptake. I miss things. So I often go onto YouTube afterwards and seek out reviews and explanations, and thereby discover all those things I failed to spot. Like plot, meaning, and character traits. I mention this because of my first trip to see a Bond movie. The film was *Diamonds Are Forever*, the year was 1971 and I came out confused. I had been struck by the scene where a group of hoodlums grabbed hold of a partially clothed woman and threw her out of a dangerously high hotel window. That was shocking. That was memorable. That was naughty. She was only partially clothed after all. And I was only eight. But apart from that I was confused. I couldn't understand a thing, and from then on I was convinced that I would never ever EVER understand a Bond plot. They were far too clever for me. Too sophisticated. Too sharp.

And so I was amazed when, 20 years later, I read *On Her Majesty's Secret Service* and ACTUALLY UNDERSTOOD IT! What? How could that be possible? It was a Bond story for goodness sake. Turns out that the movie version of *Diamonds* has a terribly contrived plot which makes about as much sense as chucking bits from five different *Postman Pat* jigsaws together and expecting to end up with the Mona Lisa. It also turns out that the seventh Bond movie was a device for bringing Sean Connery back as the great 007 (after the untimely departure of Mr Lazenby), rather than helping the viewer understand anything whatsoever of the storyline. So! Hah! I wasn't so stupid after all! Mind you, don't ask me to explain the plot of *Mamma Mia*. Now that *is* complex.

She survived by the way. In case you were worried. The partially clad woman out the window. There was a swimming pool below.

My Mates Tintin and Indy

One Christmas when I was about the age of ten a friend of my parents bought me four *Tintin* books. I loved 'em. I had seen an episode of *The Crab With The Golden Claws* on TV and it seemed to me that there was an almost mythical quality to this young adventurer in the raincoat and the blue sweater, with his quiff, his blistering barnacled bushy bearded mate Captain Haddock and his resilient white dog Snowy. I can feel that distant sensation even now. That thrill. There was something just perfect about the animation and the adventures. Technicoloured yarns that were alive with mystery

and action, tales dripping with possibilities. Our older daughter Amy has all the stories on DVD now, she too fell in love with the young Belgian hero.

In the late 70s George Lucas and Steven Spielberg sat on a beach and concocted a new hero. Just for me. ☺ When George asked Steven what film he'd make if he could do anything, Mr S said he'd like to do an old school *Boys Own* kind of adventure. And so Indiana Jones was born, with Han Solo making the role his own. Perfect. I find it hard to name my all-time favourite film, but I often say that Indy is my all-time favourite character. I'm a sucker for a bit of derring-do, with an exploding truckload of hoodlums, humour and humanity thrown in.

When I wrote The Bloke's Bible I think I tried to bring some of that derring-do to the adventures. I wanted to bring the stories off the page, flesh out the characters and draw out the humour and humanity. The heroes in the Bible make plenty of gaffs, doesn't make them any less courageous or faithful, but they get it wrong just as they get it right. And that's surely something we can all relate to. It seems to me that the worst thing we can do is imagine that all those folks in the Good Book (apart from Jesus) are two-dimensional stained glass saints. Of course they aren't. The good news of the Bible is that God is well-used to working with those who bumble and muddle along. It's all he has ever worked with. He can do extraordinary things with ordinary people. That's the glorious thing. Not that we are great. But that he is.

The Music You Love at 16

Somebody somewhere once said that the music you love at 16 you'll love forever. At 15 I loved *Showaddywaddy, Abba, Queen, Status Quo, The Beach Boys* and *The Electric Light Orchestra*. By the time I turned 16 I had fallen for *The Clash*, *The Jam*, *Stiff Little Fingers*, *Elvis Costello*, *Squeeze*, *Ian Dury and the Blockheads, The Boomtown Rats* and *Blondie*. And a girl in our drama class. To be honest the music was far more available to me than the girl in drama. But she was a punk, and loved by myself and my best mate. And so she was part of the reason we both became punk rockers.

Now hold on there, when I say *became* I don't mean we adopted bright green mohawk haircuts, stuck pins through our cheeks and wore spittle-spattered bondage trousers. From the outside you wouldn't have known a thing. But inside, where it counts (*!!*) we became die-hard rebels. Sort of. And that saying about being 16 turns out to be true. I still listen to the likes of *The Clash* and *The Jam* and *Elvis Costello*. That said I still listen to *Queen, Abba* and *The Beach Boys*. But there you go. I guess the whole *Music you love at 16* thing is not an exact science.

Punk and New Wave hit the spot for me at the right time. I loved the energy, the fast and furious nature of the tunes, the angst and rebellion expressed. Rebellion is not always a bad thing, my favourite Star Wars quote (not that I'm an expert in any way on that galaxy far far away) is this one from *Rogue One* – 'We have hope, rebellions are built on hope.' Amen. There was something about the raw energy and ragged edges of punk, I was ready for that.

I was by now at Broadoak Comprehensive in Weston-Super-Mare. Unlike Redruth it had been a comp for ten years. I seemed to manage to fit in okay, though they had already done some mathematical thing called *matrices* which I'd never heard of and, to do day, really have no idea what I'm talking about. I made some good friends though and one of them was a big fan of some group called Dr Feelgood. I know now they were a pub rock band, and highly influential in paving the way for punk.

So what of punk? Well I'm glad you asked. ☺ What I do think is that punk and Christianity have an awful lot in common. Stay with me here… Being a sucker for nostalgia I watch all the documentaries I can find about that old 1976 revolution. And in all of them there will be a moment when someone talks about seeing *The Sex Pistols* for the first time and being blown away and changed by the experience. No one had quite encountered this before, and it was totally accessible for a generation who felt outside of the previous music scene. This was a racket for the kids. And if you couldn't play a church organ or a school recorder or even the guitar, well you could have a go. You could try, you could join the fuss, leap into the kerfuffle. Make your own music. Everyone was invited, but especially the young, marginalised and disaffected.

Just like following Jesus. Very much like following Jesus. To encounter him is like nothing else on planet earth, it can blow us away and seriously change things. Like punk it can be a bit of a racket, very messy at the edges and offensive to folks with their own agendas who want to control the system. Plus we don't have to be good at being spiritual or religious. We don't have to be good at all. As I said, the disaffected, marginalised and young are especially invited to take part. And as we do, like so many of those scruffy young guitar heroes, we learn as we go. One chord at a time. One song at a time. One rebel yell at a time.

And if there is one thing that seems clearer to me with each passing day it's this, Jesus is the purest, most radical rebel ever. The one bucking the system and side-stepping the trends. He's not bothered about popularity or pleasing people or building his empire or effective marketing campaign. He's out there doing his own thing. Still. Like a busker in ripped jeans, strumming a beat-up old guitar and singing a heart-warming protest song. Seeing how many people will set aside their agendas for a moment to hear the music from another place. Or to quote a *Buzzcocks* album title – *Another Music In a Different Kitchen*.

Frank and Romeo

I started attending a midweek youth club at the local Baptist church after befriending some of the guys on a youth weekend. We listened to a lot of raw and angsty music there, bantered about this and that, and fell in and out of love with the various girls. Nothing ever happened of course. I secretly fell in and out of love with various girls from my own church too. But I couldn't quite imagine cutting the mustard when it came to 'being a boyfriend'. I didn't know what was expected, what you said, how you behaved. I dreamt of being a great Romeo Montague but in reality was closer to Frank Spencer. When I was finally shoved into asking someone out by a friend the thing lasted about two weeks and nothing ever really took place in that time. I didn't know how you did the relationship thing. It was a foreign land to me.

Eventually, at 17 I fell for someone and we did have a relationship for a few months. This was one of many that I stumbled through in the next couple of years. I felt that I never acquitted myself that well and I think I began to develop a fear of commitment. Though I didn't know that at the time. I loved the first rush of starting a relationship and threw myself in headlong, but didn't do so well when it came to the long run and hanging in there.

Darts

Songs are powerful. And I've always loved them. There is a great scene in the film *Music and Lyrics* where Hugh Grant's character, a songwriter, explains about the power of a three minute pop song to Drew Barrymore. He tells her that all the novels in the world can't make you feel so good so quickly as a line like, 'I've got sunshine on a cloudy day, when it's cold outside, I've got the month of May...' from the Temptations' song *My Girl*. And I'm with him on that. Pop music has played in the wings of my life ever since I can remember. The likes of *The Drifters, The Beach Boys, Showaddywaddy, Queen, Abba, ELO, Blondie, The Clash, The Jam, The Alarm, Bruce Springsteen, The Specials, The Beat, The Beautiful South, Scouting for Girls* and plenty of others have brightened my days and urged me on.

I can often tell you where I was, what I was doing and even sometimes how I was feeling by referencing a song from the time. I can hear a song and it takes me right back to a particular time or experience. Likewise I can often work out what age I was at a given time by remembering which songs were in the charts at that particular moment in my history. For example, a whole fistful of New Wave numbers takes me right back to those halcyon 1979 days when I was leaving school and about to start a full time job.

One of my persistently happy memories is of playing darts with my dad in our hallway one evening with Blondie's vinyl single *Heart of Glass* playing on repeat in the background. You just had to lift up the stacking arm on our record player and the disc would play forever. No idea who won the darts but I think I'll always remember the joy of that experience. My last day at school I came home to find two albums, the Eagles' *Hotel California* and Dr Feelgood's *Down by the Jetty*, waiting for me in the hall. The day I bought my first hi-fi system I also bought Bill Lovelady's *Reggae for it Now* and played it to death on my new turntable, blasting out of the speakers my dad had fixed to my bedroom wall. When I went on a weeklong trip with our church youth group we spent the week singing 10cc's *Dreadlock Holiday* and *Summer Nights* from the musical Grease. When I hear *Somebody to Love* by Queen I'm back in a lunchtime classroom on a Tuesday in 1977, listening to the charts on a tiny transistor radio and feeling heartbroken that it hasn't made it to number one.

These things may mean nothing much to you. It may well be another kind of music that warms your ears, but I'm glad of the gift of it, and often say that though we have 150 songs smack in the middle of the Bible we don't know whether the tunes were like those of Abba, Led Zeppelin, Bach or Andrew Lloyd Webber. Or any other artist. Whatever, I say it again, songs are powerful and they colour our worlds.

Beach Baby

Lately I've been listening again to a clutch of songs from the 70s, and one has particular power to transport me back. It is, I admit, not a classic, but that's not the point. It's tied to a specific experience in such a graphic way as to grip me by the collar and whisk me right back in time whenever I hear it, faster than any plutonium-powered DeLorean.

This particular song takes me back to 1974, and the tender age of 11. In '74 I left junior school in my home village of Illogan, and moved up to Redruth Grammar school. In my early days there I recall a dark, powerful, haunting moment, linked with a surprisingly cheesy, happy song. I was in a queue for something or other, football socks or some highly invasive inoculative injection, the kind of thing we got as new intakes in the mid 70s.

Across the corridor, in another line of boys, one young chap spotted the approach of a slightly older boy and broke into song. *Beach Baby* by First Class. Remember that classic? I'm sure you do. You know. That one. About the beach. And the baby. I'm whistling it right now for you. No? Oh well, there's always YouTube… It was a happy summer disco number. About hanging about on the sand picking up girls. Totally pc. The song contained a reference to the name of the guy approaching, and whether he had a particular grievance against the singer, or whether he was just fed up of people singing this song as he passed by I don't know. But he lunged himself at the younger boy, gripped his face in his hand and shoved it back against the wall, hard, uttering a threat of some kind or other.

I had never seen such violence before, such vicious intent. The abrupt and raw nature of the attack made something in me flinch and recoil. There were no punches thrown, no knives or bottles in evidence, but the manner of the onslaught was enough. It sickened me. Opened my eyes to a kind of anger I had not seen in my young 11 years. No damage was done and it was all over in a few seconds. But forever more that song was destined to take me back to that corridor in 1974, and the capability of people to want to hurt one another for seemingly trivial reasons.

Climb Every... Climbing Wall

I've never been that good at any kind of sport. I don't find co-ordination that easy. And as I mentioned before, being a writer I much prefer living in my head. I once got good at table tennis – a remarkable feat for someone like me. An anti-sportsperson actually mastering something. It only happened because there was a table tennis table in the bank I stared working in back in 1979. And there was a friend working there called Steve, who was great at table tennis and quite happy to give me a 20 point lead when he played me. (If you don't know you only need 21 points to win, so I was chasing a single point.) I still lost. Time after time.

But after a while I started – shock! – winning. I managed to win that elusive point, and so the lead came down to 15 points, then down to 10 then five. And suddenly I was starting to beat him from zero. Well, not suddenly, this followed weeks and months of staying back after work to bash ten bells out of a ping pong ball together. If Steve had offered to coach me and give me lessons I'd have run a mile. But he wasn't that kind of guy. So he just let me play badly... until I could play quite well. I'll always be grateful for that.

But to wind the clock back further a moment, we had a climbing wall in the sports hall at Redruth Comprehensive school. And one day, somewhere around the age of 13, I found myself halfway up there. I didn't just wake up and discover myself roped up and clinging on… I'd been sent up there because 'it was my turn'. Oh! Really? Great?! Halfway up I gave up the ghost, and any attempt at dignity, and yelled down to my teacher that I couldn't go on. I would fall and break a million bones. And no doubt leave a crater the size of the O2 in the sports hall floor. I was sure of it. Please, please, PLEASE sir… can I come down now? No. Of course I couldn't. I was there to climb the wall.

However, my teacher turned out to be a human being after all. And a wise one at that. 'You see that next level above you? Just go up to that one,' he called. I looked up to the platform a little above me. Could I do that? Could I? Maybe? Perhaps? Turns out I could, and at breakneck speed too. I shot up that wall, reached the target and was back on solid ground before you could say Sherpa Tenzing Norgay.

And I think, I hope, I learned something that day. About setting achievable goals. A couple of years back I was speaking at an army chaplain college. And some of the guys were telling stories about their experiences of helping the soldiers. One of them told of a guy who had come to him during basic training, one of the hardest periods in a soldier's life, and said he was giving up. The chaplain asked him to set a goal. What would he like to achieve? Completing the training, the solider replied. No, no, that's way too much. Instead, the chaplain said, tell you what – make it through to tomorrow lunchtime and come back and see me again. Small steps. Achievable goals. Worth hanging on to.

I often travel back in time to that climbing wall, not sure how often I stick to the achievable goals thing, but I remember making it to just the next level. A wise move when the going is hard.

+ + +

Before leaving Cornwall I got confirmed. I hadn't wanted to, as going to classes meant cycling past a group of local corner-boy skinheads of an evening. But I plucked up the courage and made the effort. At one of the preparation meetings the rector described how he had walked outside one night, looked up at the stars and committed his life to God. I so wanted to do this but kept quiet. I was too afraid it might be emotional, and thereby embarrassing.

The bishop turned up for the confirmation service, as bishops tend to do, and I went forward and knelt with the others. As the bishop placed his hands on my head I got this sudden feeling that I was going to cry. Something powerful was going on. I went back to my seat and kept my head bowed for a long time until my composure was back intact.

You're My Best Friend

Another song memory – a happier one, and one of the few school assembly recollections I have, though it has nothing to do with what was being presented to us from the front. At the time I was a big Queen fan and as we loitered towards the back of the hall (I think I was in the fifth year at the time, what we now laughingly call year 11. Sorry. I cannot get my head around the maths of it. Just call me Fuddy closely followed by Duddy.)

Anyway there we were, wishing the half hour away when all of a sudden... could it be true? Yep. The distant strains of Queen's classic *You're my best friend* came drifting in from the great beyond. Was the headmaster a closet Queen fan? Who knew? All I know is that my mate Simon gave me a knowing smile and something about that moment lifted my spirits. And let's face it, there are moments in school assemblies when you really need your spirits lifted.

When I later went on to present school assemblies as part of various Christian groups my aim was always to offer something that connected with the kids, whether it was referencing pop music, TV programmes or something else cultural for them. My view is if you connect Jesus with the latest chart tune then the next time the kids hear it, well... they may make the connection again. Or if not then, they may later make the connection as they grow up.

Pier Pressure

Do you ever replay scenarios in your head? I do it all the time. Think about what I should have done after the fact. Wish I could go back and tidy up something I've done or said.

Weston-Super-Mare has a pier. It famously burned down and got rebuilt a few years ago. One afternoon, towards the end of my years at school I was loitering on there with a friend. (That was unusual for me, wandering around town was more my thing.) My mate was chatting to a friend of his, who I didn't know. I don't recall the conversation but I do remember that this mate of his pointed across the pier to a young woman we didn't know and challenged me to go over and ask her out!

Of course he knew I wouldn't do it, and I knew I wouldn't do it, and he knew I knew I wouldn't do it etc. But all these years later, in a corner of my mind where I'm James Bond, I rethink the scenario and I wish I'd had the courage to go over to her and say something like, 'Look, this guy over there challenged me to come over and ask you out, so could you do me a favour and just smile and nod at me and then forget about it. Or even better just scribble some random digits on my hand with this pen as if you're giving me your number.'

She might have punched my lights out of course, or had me arrested, but on the other hand I might have been able to bluff my way and look cool. Which raises a question as to why it matters. In reality I ended up feeling inadequate and foolish. Not a proper 'lad about town'. Which hurts when you're young and impressionable. As if somehow the ability to saunter about like Casanova was the height of maturity. The guy on the pier has probably never thought twice about it since. And yet here I am, tapping keys and telling the story. I so wish I'd had the courage, and the mental agility, to be able to tell you a different story. But then, I wouldn't be me would I. I'd be Simon Templar or some other suave and sophisticated fictional hero.

The way I measure success is so often flawed. Governed by what others think of me. It's something I constantly battle with, wanting to please people and impress them, forgetting that little tiny detail about what God thinks of me. How he cherishes me and wants to nourish my longings and insecurities.

'Where your heart is...' Jesus once said, 'that's where your treasure will be.' I want to set my heart on God's heart, but it keeps wandering off, meandering away like a curious puppy, or a restless wasp. Looking for meaning in the wrong places.

Cut Cocoon

As recently mentioned, I don't recall many of the things I was told in school assemblies. I do remember the hymn sheets at primary school. Thick wads of cream coloured paper suspended from strings that the teachers lowered so they could flip the pad until *Morning Has Broken* or *Fight the Good Fight* appeared. Who needs a touch screen when you have thick unwieldy pads of worship songs?

One school assembly does stick in my mind though. Or rather, one story told at a school assembly. About a cocoon. And the way that someone sat watching a butterfly struggle to break out into a new life. The person watching thought they would lend a hand, make it easier, so they took a knife and carefully enlarged the hole. The butterfly broke through sooner... no doubt about that... less struggle... but! The creature turned out improperly formed. It's a sad tale. Helping the thing change too quickly had impeded its growth. I guess it shows the power of a good story. Here I am writing about it all these years later. Change is slow, painful, a struggle. Not easy. And often the struggle of the journey is as important as the destination.

I love all kinds of stories, especially films. But books too, and Jesus's parables. I read recently that if you hear a story with a meaning and think you have understood it, then think again! Be careful that your comprehension of it doesn't kill it. Parables are alive. They should go on knocking at the doors of our head, hearts, and wills. To think we have grasped a story does not necessarily mean we have forged it into our daily living.

Jesus drew on all kinds of sources for his tales. When he told his prodigal son story he was referencing the crucial tale of Jacob and Esau. When he spoke of an unpopular king going away on a trip and leaving responsibilities behind he was drawing on a recent real life news story. Jesus knew the power of a cultural reference to help folk remember and connect. Next time you read the great banquet and folks refusing to pitch up, imagine Kate and Will's royal wedding, and the streets empty because no one wants a part of it.

I recently saw one of Jesus's stories in a whole new light when I heard a talk on it. A servant takes his master's money and starts slashing debtor's bills. He took money and used it for good. That's one of the meanings of Jesus's story in Luke 16. Use unrighteous mammon to bless others. Jesus of course lived this out. He was supported by Joanna, amongst others, and she got her cash from her husband Chuza who worked for bad lad Pharaoh. Jesus happily received her gifts and turned them for God. He never feared contamination, but rather turned to good all he touched.

In the Money

I got my first job at the tender age of 15. Four hours on a Saturday night, 5 till 9, selling petrol in a local garage earning 50p an hour. Luxury! If you'd have told me a year before that I'd be doing this I would have been horrified. But moving to Weston had brought me out of my shell. I'd made good friends with a group my age at church. We hung around a lot together and it helped me to start growing up. I learnt about all kinds of things from them, how to tell the best jokes, where to buy the local chips, how to fall in and out of love. That sort of thing.

In my last year at school I went to see the careers officer. He asked me what I wanted to do with my life. I said I wanted to be a journalist, I'm not sure I really meant that, but it was the writer in me sneaking out. This was something I kept quiet, along with my belief in God. You didn't want to go telling the people things like the truth at places like school. At least that's what I figured anyway. The careers officer looked at me, said something about it not being the easiest of jobs and suggested I try banking. So I did. I wrote off to NatWest, Lloyds and another, maybe TSB and only had a reply from one. NatWest gave me an interview, I prayed with my parents about it and suddenly bingo. I was in. My place in banking history secured. Five years of making oceans of coffee, counting cash, punching a huge computer keyboard, making silly mistakes, going clubbing, having a laugh... here we come.

I was in the money. Not much of it my own. But there you go. I was free and independent. The first thing I did with my first pay-cheque was buy a hi-fi system. Now that's prioritising for you.

I had a lot of good times in NatWest Oxford Street. Made a lot of good friends too, and sometimes overstepped the mark. When an edict came down from on high that we should all stipulate carefully any funds we paid into our accounts I thought this was ridiculous and petty. So in an act of defiance, when I next had some money to pay in I recorded it on the slip as *Bank Raid Loot*! Ha ha, that'll get them rolling in the aisles. Unfortunately the manager did not share my sense of humour, and when he spotted it the next day his cheerful response was, 'What the bloody hell's this?'

Oops. Just a joke sir. I don't recall him laughing.

On the subject of my writing, I don't think I told others in the bank about my aspirations. Perhaps I had discarded them by then. The only time I had let it slip at school was when we had a supply teacher one day who was chatting to myself and a girl in, I think, a French class. The teacher asked what we did, and astonishingly I told her I wrote stories. The memory stands out to me because I kept my desire to write so quiet. These days if I can I try and encourage others to keep writing, even secretly.

Messy

My conversion is messy. It doesn't follow the usual paths. Especially when you bear in mind I had grown up in a Christian home, always believed in God and two of my favourite books were Christian biographies *Run Baby Run* and *Miracle on the River Kwai*. The thing was all the bits were there… just not in the right order, as Eric Morecambe might say.

I had always been to church with my family, my parents were deeply caring and devoted people who had themselves always gone to church, my father being a server in the choir as a boy. So from the word go my life was infused with Christian things. My dad prayed with me each night as he tucked me up in bed. My one early memory of Stoke church is of attending an evening service with my dad, I was probably about four or five, the building seemed dark and chilly and huge, and there was a choir. To this day when I hear some choral piece I am back there, small and bright-eyed in the half-light of that massive building. Beside my lovely dad.

In Cornwall we attended the local parish church in the village, my sister and I both ended up in the choir. One of my earliest recollections is of playing a shepherd in a nativity scene, decked out in all the truly rural costume befitting the character, i.e. a dressing gown and tea towel.

But I was conflicted. I held tightly to my belief in God, it was vital to me, an intrinsic part of my being, like it was in my DNA. And yet I was terrified about telling others I believed in God, I didn't want to be belittled, or to upset them, or something somewhere in between the two. So I spent my school years keeping it well under wraps. Compartmentalising that vital part of me. I still struggle with it now. Something to do with being a private person and not wanting to upset people's feelings. Though I didn't know any of that at the time. I think that's why I love the possibilities and the reach offered by the internet now. You can write something and put it out there and you never know how far it will go and where it might land. Like the farmer in Jesus's tale, throwing out the seed and letting it go to land in all kinds of soil. You're offering something with an open hand and it is up to people to take it or not. Consider it or not. And there's great freedom in letting it go so God can do his thing with it. I love that.

Rumours and Floating

Having up-sticked to Weston in 1977, my sister and I returned to Illogan early in 1980. We stayed with a friend for a long weekend and I encountered a few key things. Firstly a couple of albums, *Monty Python Live at Drury Lane* which I found hilarious. And along with it *Rumours* by Fleetwood Mac. Not so hilarious but I loved it from the moment the needle hit the vinyl. I had heard talk of both of these at school and no doubt played along as if I was in the know, but once again I was a late starter. I fell in love with both Python and *Rumours*.

But something far more influential took place. We hooked up with our old mates from Illogan church who were going to hear the great David Watson speak in Truro Cathedral on the Sunday evening. So I was worried. I was scared it would be all emotional and overwhelming. It wasn't. Well, it was but not in the way I imagined. David had brought Riding Lights with him and so this was my first experience of seeing Christian drama. The group did a sketch called *Light of the World* – I can still remember it after all these years. That's the power of good drama for ya. I also remember a joke David told (no time to tell it now, sorry, email me) and… at the end of the meeting, I felt as if I was floating. Seriously.

I was sitting in my seat quietly praying, and for the first time I started thanking God for who he was…

and it happened. This incredible feeling of wellbeing, which I can only describe as floating. When we returned home the following evening I told my dad and he prayed for me to be filled with the Holy Spirit. And I cried. And spoke in tongues. And felt like I was floating again. So there you have it. I still wasn't sure if I was a proper Christian. And I still didn't want to tell anyone about it. But I could speak in tongues and had experienced the power of God. Just goes to show he won't be confined by our tidy theological boxes I guess.

The next day I went back to work in NatWest, where there were two other Christians working. One of them offered me a lift home after work and on the way – I kid you not – asked me if I could speak in tongues!!! Seriously! How about that for timing? I said that I sort of could, hedging my bets I guess, and he told me that I either could or I couldn't. I think God was on my case with no intention whatsoever of giving up.

A Very Big House in the Country

There is a large country house on the edge of Exmoor, just outside the village of Lynton in North Devon. At one time a rich guy called Squire Bailey owned it, then a million other things happened, the decades rolled by and the church bought it for a mere pittance. Well, £28,000, but it's a mere pittance for a 300 acre oil painting estate with a hulk of a house on it. My parents stayed there for a holiday in May 1980 and they decided to return in the autumn with their son in tow.

The months had passed and I was still keeping shtum about my faith. Living a kind of double life. Then I went with my parents to a weird place called Lee Abbey. The night before I went out on the town and drank too much so I was not in the best of health that day. Plus my parents were not sure how I'd get on. They were worried I might not fit in. They needn't have bothered. The place grabbed me like an enthusiastic rottweiler, and from the word go I fell in love with the rocks and the sea and the house and the grass and… oh every bit of it really.

From the moment I checked in I felt at home, met some great new friends and had the time of my life. Till one of my new friends asked me if I'd ever made a commitment, a definite decision to live as a Christian. I didn't intend to come clean, but Dennis asked me while we were out jogging together and as

I'm not a jogger I wasn't thinking straight and he caught me unawares. So I didn't mean to tell the truth but found myself saying, 'No.' He told me to think about it and the next day there I was praying with him in the Lee Abbey chapel. It was a deeply moving and profound experience. And yet, and yet... when I returned to the bank I fluffed my first chance to tell folks what had happened and then lost my nerve. I was on a second week of holiday but popped in to have a cuppa with my friends there. Steve, my table tennis playing mate, asked me where I'd been the week before. This was it. The moment of truth. I bit the bullet and went for it.

'A Christian community called Lee Abbey.'

At least that was the gist of my answer. And of course everything was all right. Or... no it wasn't... life is complex isn't it? It hangs by a slender thread, turns on a sixpence sometimes and major decisions are made in the briefest of moments. The reason I'm not exactly sure what I said to Steve is because something else happened as I told him. Maybe the kettle boiled, maybe someone else called out, maybe a meteorite crashed through the window. Who knows? What I do know is that he looked away and missed my reply, and by the time we resumed the conversation he had forgotten the question and I didn't have the courage to repeat my answer. The moment passed and there I was, floundering... back to normality for another year. Yes! Another year! Keeping shtum and going nowhere.

Take 2

I returned to Lee Abbey a year after my first visit, again with my parents. The year in between had been random and chaotic, I felt as if I was a bit lost, drinking too much sometimes (I even pitched up at work on one afternoon worse for wear after a pub lunch). I was confused about my faith, and probably a little frustrated about things in general.

So I went back to the big house in the country for a second holiday. Doing my usual compartmentalising thing I was able to put my normal life on hold and throw myself into the wonders of that glorious place for another week. The year before I had met and befriended a guy called Simon, and we had agreed to meet up again on that same week. And that changed everything.

Simon was different, he had changed. Like me he had made a fresh commitment to God the previous year and it had impacted him. I could see that. And likewise I knew I hadn't changed a bit. I was drifting, I'd made a commitment when Dennis prayed for me but I was still the same old dubious Dave.

And that was it. Simon's life transformed. That's what clinched it for me and gave me the shove I needed. When I returned to the bank I told everyone, and my life took a whole new turn.

Chocolates

Not long after returning from my second trip to Lee Abbey I was befriended by a great Christian guy Andy, and as a result we met Mike, who was starting a *Youth For Christ* movement in Weston. The night we met Mike was extraordinary. We were attending a local churches youth event, and we planned to stand up at the end and announce that we were starting a band (Andy) and a drama group (me). We were just about to speak up when Mike stood and announced he was starting a local *Youth For Christ* group and he was looking for volunteers to do music and drama! We nearly fell through the floor. Timing or what??

I had only recently started doing drama after seeing mime artist Geoffrey Stevenson in Bristol. I found that the memory of the mime he performed, about eating chocolates and getting stuck in the box, kept rattling around my head. Then when our church youth group leader, Alan, told me we needed to present something at a forthcoming youth event I told him about the mime. He asked me to do it there and then, no rehearsal or anything, so I did! And he said, 'You can do that then!' The extraordinary thing was that Alan was a drama teacher! So he knew about such things. That impromptu performance, and Alan's encouragement, changed my life. Amazing too when you think that I had failed my drama O level!

I bought a couple of Christian drama books written by *Riding Lights Theatre Company*, and these gave me my initial ideas and material. We fell about laughing at the jokes and humorous dialogues. I'd never realised you could tell Bible stories in this entertaining way. But it was Mike at *Youth For Christ* who gave me my first piece of inspiration for writing my own drama sketch. He'd had this idea about a scenario where God had a secretary. And you couldn't just talk to him straight, you had to go through various bits of comical red tape. We called it *If God Was a Civil Servant*, and it was the start of something big for me. Biblical drama sketches.

I knew nothing about drama but bluffed and blundered my way. I started the two groups, one in our church and one with *Youth For Christ.* At 18 I was convinced I could conquer the world. I watched Geoffrey Stevenson do a few more mimes and nicked them all as well. They were heady days. Exciting times, we tried lots of things, sometimes fell flat on our faces. But learned so much. *Youth For Christ* didn't transform Weston, but we did plenty of good things and motivated a number of young people. We did two big concerts in our local Tech and various other outreach events. I was blown away when an American theatre company pitched up and presented the magical *Toymaker and Son*. A brilliantly creative allegory that would inspire me for years to come.

The closing months of 1981 proved to be busy ones. Not long after my life changed at Lee Abbey, and I got busy doing drama, I also passed my driving test which meant I was now mobile, so could ferry my new YFC friends around for events and meetings. My sister Liz got married to Martin that year too. My big sister with her own house and husband. It was one of those key years really, a lot happening.

I was in my third year of working in the bank at that point and I used to sit on the till scribbling away, writing sketches between counting the fivers. Shoving the drama scripts out of sight whenever a customer appeared at the window. Having come clean about my new faith I went at it with a certain amount of gusto. I wanted to convert everyone now, whether they liked it or not! I kicked up quite a dust storm in the branch for a while.

I returned to Lee Abbey again in '82 and in '83 applied to join the community there. I went for an interview in the snowy depths of January and got all fired up for a new life. Then I came home and got the rejection letter and had to readjust. They felt that I should stick at my work and the various drama projects I was doing. So, after some initial disappointment, I did.

I continued at the bank, calmer now, and the heated religious debates I had sparked fizzled out. Instead I met once a week with the other two Christians in the branch, Ann and Murray, and we prayed together for the other members of staff. I was still outspoken and at times defensive about my faith, but things had changed a lot, and coming out of the closet about my faith had turned my life in a whole new direction. I gave up drinking alcohol (I often relied on it to overcome my shyness when we went out clubbing) and took the posters of Ian Dury, Debbie Harry and The Damned off my bedroom wall. I also stopped keeping a record of the weekly top 40 singles charts, something I had done for the previous five years. When a friend from church came round one night I pointed at my fairly sizeable album collection and said something like, 'Help yourself.' Not sure if her eyes popped but they may well have done.

In!

There is a set of stone steps right by a cliff edge on the Lee Abbey estate. Just below a path known as Jenny's Leap. The spot overlooks the sea and the view is breathtaking. I had gone there on the last day of my second trip to Lee Abbey in 1981, the day before returning home to tell everyone I was a Christian. As I stood there a gentle breeze started shifting the branches in a tree near my face and I got a sudden sense of God's gentle presence. And with that, an assurance that I would one day go into some kind of full time Christian work. I had no idea what. But I just knew that I would. One of those things that's hard to put into words. There was no voice in the sky or anything like that. Just the affirming sense of God's presence.

Now it was 1984. Two and a half years had gone by. Had I misread that call? Was it just wishful thinking? At the end of one of our evening services I went forward to pray with our minister Malcolm. I told him I needed some guidance, but I was willing to stay in the bank if that was what I should do. Without batting an eyelid he said, 'I've always thought you should be at Lee Abbey.' I reapplied, not knowing if you were allowed to do that. They told me they currently had no vacancies but as I was due to go for an Easter break I could chat to John the warden then. I went for Easter. I chatted to John. I went home and received a letter saying that unexpectedly some community members were leaving. I was in. I was going to work at Lee Abbey!

I left the bank on 10th August 1984. In my five years of full time working I had learned to type, make coffee, count fivers very quickly, play table tennis, answer the phone all businesslike (and in those days you had to say the full title *National Westminster Bank*, none of this shoddy NatWest lark), and had donned a white beard and red robe to become a rather too skinny Father Christmas each festive season. More importantly I had made some great friends, had a lot of good times, and become a Christian. I'm tempted to say I had grown up, but that would be stretching it.

Ten days later I threw a good proportion of my worldly goods in the Renault I had bought a while back from Anne, one of my Christian friends in the bank, and I said an emotional goodbye to my mum and dad. The raw farewell caught me off-guard, one of those moments when I suddenly felt the world shifting beneath my feet a little. I had been so excited about my new plan, now I was faced with the reality of it. I was leaving home. Yikes. Would it be all right? We hugged and I pulled out into slow-moving summer traffic.

Not The Two Ronnies

Homesickness hit me on that very first day. Everyone seemed so happy and popular and confident, and they all knew each other, and they didn't know me! Everyone was welcoming but still, this was like another world.

It didn't last long. I went for a walk that afternoon to Jenny's Leap, sat on the bench there and looked at the name badge my community 'dad' Jon had given to me. It said David. (I hadn't yet morphed into Dave, though I would soon.) I flipped it over. Written on the back was the very same Bible verse that I had been given a few months previously. 'I know the plans I have for you, plans to prosper you, not to harm you.' It's from Jeremiah chapter 29 verse 11, and I had been given it at Easter when I came for my interview. Maybe things would be all right after all. Within a day I was starting to feel a part of the life there.

I had always struggled with compartmentalising my life, still do really. As a teenager I had kept my school friends separate from my church friends. Somehow I found it disturbing to bring the two together, what if they didn't like each other? What if it exposed me in some way? Not least my stumbling belief in God. I mention this because one of the advantages of working at Lee Abbey was that it brought all the parts of my life together. Work, social, spiritual, meals, friends, home. It blurred the lines between the compartments, and helped with the temptation to cover the cracks with a happy face at Sunday church or the weekly home group. We saw each other on good days and bad. Early in the morning and late at night. Gleeful and grumpy. When cleaning loos and chasing pigs. Covered in food waste and farm waste. All these things helped me to be a little more genuine with the community I lived with and the guests who came each week.

We also had a shedload of fun. I was conscripted into a four-man garden team, surprising for an ex-bank clerk, but don't let that fool you. We were a creative quartet and were just as likely to be making up a new comedy routine to perform to the guests as we were digging spuds or pulling leeks.

We were big fans of the then popular Two Ronnies and my gardening mate Chris taught me a lot about how to concoct comedy material. I often look back on my first year there as the time of my single life. The possibilities were endless. I sang lead in *The Gatecrashers* punk band, and played the tea chest in a spoof rockabilly group *The Loons*. I impersonated Stan Laurel, John Travolta, Eric Liddell and Marcel Marceau. We were the new kings of comedy. Nothing could could stop us. We rewrote such classics as *My Brother, As Time Goes By, Singing in the Rain, Raindrops Keep Falling on My Head* and *Summer Nights*.

The Gatecrashers and the rockabilly Loons.

Chris and I also drew on various classics of the stage and screen. During one entertainment evening I walked on, laid down a sheet of newspaper and stood on it. Chris then walked in and mimed stabbing me in the back. We looked at the audience, grinned and announced, 'Murder on the Daily Express!' Later one of us ran in with one eye shut, hunting high and low, till the other ran in, clutching a fake eye and calling, 'Jed, Jed! I got it!'. A grin at the audience as we announced, 'The Return of Jed's Eye.' At another moment Chris sidled up to me in a long coat, pulled out a tennis racket, and surreptitiously sold it to me. He walked off and I gleefully said, 'The merchant of tennis.' Appalling eh? But we loved 'em. Had as much fun making them up as performing them. Along with fellow gardeners Richard and Kevin.

Our writing career began because Richard's birthday was fast approaching. At our four o'clock tea break we started penning a song, based on old classics rewritten, and before we knew it we had revamped a number of old songs and missed the last forty minutes of work. It was the shape of things to come.

One of the rewrites was *Messing About on the River*...

'When you can't find no one, and there's work to be done, he'll be messing about in the greenhouse... With strawberries to weed and flowers to pot, you just mention work and he's off like a shot! They say he ain't smart, but the moment we start, he goes messing about in the greenhouse.'

Along with an old harvest number...

'He ploughs the fields and splatters the cow dung on the ground, but his aim ain't too brilliant he spreads it all around. We know we're into sharing to give beyond our call, but with his generosity he tends to cover all. All the lads around us are caked from head to toe, before we get another load I think we'd better go.'

Chris, Kev and I did get up to rather a lot of practical joking in my first year –

- Whilst potting a load of plants in the greenhouse we noticed that damp peat has a rather similar consistency to that of warm chocolate brownies, so we cut some neat slices, trayed them up and took them down to the tea break. We intervened when one of the kitchen team came dangerously close to trying one
- On 14th February we grabbed a stack of old Christmas cards, rewrote them for Valentine's Day and sent one to every female on the community, it went down rather well actually
- We snuck into Alan the chaplain's room and turned all the furniture upside down, that didn't go down so well actually
- Unbeknown to the director we rewrote an entire scene in the Christmas pantomime, substituting the fairy godmother with a mafia-like fairy godfather (we thought it'd be hilarious to spring it on everyone!). The director was Alan the chaplain again, he was very patient with us.

Cabin Fever

There was once a little toll hut, sheltering beside a road under a spreading leafy tree. Singer Adrian Snell talks happily of his time spent there, he wrote at least one of his fine tunes while collecting coins from the passing vehicles. He spent a happy summer there and so did I. More than one actually.

Not at the same time as Adrian, he'd passed that way years before me, and we didn't actually live in the hut. It was merely there for work purposes. You pulled out a chair, a reel of tickets and your money box, grabbed a good book and a Walkman (cassettes

in them days) and sat in the sun happily robbing the cars that passed by. The road was owned by Lee Abbey and as such needed to finance the upkeep.

I think it's fair to assume those shorts are illegal now.
And look! An extortionate 20p for the toll!

I closed out my first week at Lee Abbey with a morning stint in that old shed. I couldn't believe it. Here I was sitting in the great outdoors, the sun up in the sky, eating a cream tea provided by the fantastic tea cottage team. Perfect. And I was getting paid for it. Okay, not quite so much as when I was in the bank, but it was fair exchange. I wrote one of my more enduring sketches in that shed. *Praying is like breathing*. I pinched the phrase from David Watson and explored the idea in a short hopefully comedic sketch in which people only spent time breathing on Sunday mornings and for an hour every Wednesday night. I may well have written other classics in there too. Probably on various rainy days.

Lee Abbey really accelerated my sketch writing. And it taught me to write pieces that were visual and easy to learn as we were often given short notice and had little time for prep between pulling leeks and brushing loos. With guests arriving each week and new themes to explore there was always the need for fresh material. That said, we were also able to re-use a lot of pieces too. In my time at Lee Abbey I also came up with the idea of response stories. Interactive readings which included six repeated keywords that prompted a response, noise, or action from the audience. They were easy to present and required little preparation. CPAS published three collections of these over the years and I still find myself writing the occasional one all this time later.

A couple of years into my time a friend suggested I think about compiling my material into book form. I'd approached publishers and had no luck so the idea was a bit of a dream come true. Lee Abbey had not long installed a computer system and so my mate taught me the basics and before you could say

Bill-Shakespeare-Must-Be-Worried I was holding an A4 spiral bound copy of 28 pieces in my hand. So many good things have come out of my connection with Lee Abbey. And the drama books I produced certainly grew from my time there.

Later, in the 1990s, as result of doing my own collections of dramas, Church House Publishing and CPAS both contacted me looking to publish my material. It was a great moment when I held the first published collection of sketches in my hand. *Acting Up* – a proper book! Bound and everything! With pages and a cover!

Back at Lee Abbey in the '80s estate work continued to be a source of hard work and inspiration. We dug a lot of holes and filled them in again. That was how our boss, Richard, described gardening. It was Richard who encouraged us to keep on coming up with the madcap songs and sketches for the guests.

We planted strawberries, leeks, tomatoes, potatoes, onions, carrots and carnations. Then we picked strawberries, leeks, tomatoes, potatoes, onions, carrots and carnations. We also cut lawns. Lots of lawns. And drove daffodil the blue dumper, round and round, to our hearts' content.

Three of us gardeners doing what we did best.

We also fell in and out and in and out of love. Well I did anyway. I was a bit of an emotional nightmare on legs. I was terrified of commitment, though I didn't realise that back then. But needless to say, I didn't acquit myself very nobly at times. I remember a group of us squashed into the Warden's lounge one evening, watching the very last episode of *MASH*. In that programme one of the guys makes a farewell speech and emotionally announces that he has loved them all. His mate then stands up and says something like, 'I haven't loved you all, but I got around to as many as I could.'

I just want to say, it wasn't quite like that.

I stayed at Lee Abbey for four years, and over time my role as drama director increased to the point where I went part-time on the estate team and was given half the week to expand the role.

I loved the way that we were able to do spiritual drama alongside regular comedy stuff. One day we might be doing a dramatisation of Ezekiel's Valley of Dry Bones, the next we'd be ripping off classics from *Grease* in order to advertise pot plant sales.

Rather like this –

'Summer Plants, lovely and green, some are dying, not easily seen… Sell me more, sell me more! Do they cost very much?' … 'We got plants, they're multiplying, and we're losing control, and the flowers your supplying, they're electrifying. You'd better queue up, 'cause you need a plant, and there's one here just for you… They're the ones that you want… the ones that you want, want, oooh ooh ooh.'

I believe John Travolta was shaking in his boots.

Friends

I learnt so much from others in those four years, not least from John and Gay Perry, the leaders of the community. They were so good at caring for others, and invested in us as a community. They and their family showed us so much about what it meant to be generous and welcoming. I worked with one of their sons Tim for several months, and as well as digging holes and filling them in again we did a lot of fun stuff together too. Tim came up with a great routine involving him being a ventriloquist dummy sat on my knee. He could then say anything he liked and it looked as if I was making him say it! Tim was so full of life and enthusiasm, and like his parents, always interested in others. We continued to be friends after our Lee Abbey days.

I made so many great friends in that time on the community, I apologise for not mentioning them all, but here are just a few…

Chris, Kev, Richard, Jean, Andy, Ali, Stephen, Julia, Nige, Nigel, Jon, Tim, Simon, Mark, Charles, Clare, Jo, Suzanne, Bridget, Alan, David, Jonny, Clive, Katherine, Rich, Soobie, Chris, Nigel, Drew, Toby, Anna, Caroline, Cathy, Jenny, Annet, Craig, Jill, Sarah, Suzie, Rachel, Sally, Rosie, Rory, Peter.

So many great friends. So many great times. We laughed and cried together, learned, grew, messed about, played practical jokes, overstepped the mark, burned the candle at both ends, prayed, sang, partied, questioned, lazed, argued, bantered, danced, performed, had haircuts, cooked, hatched plots, worked, ate too much cake, sunbathed in the summer, froze in the winter and got soaked on the many occasions it rained.

Lee Abbey is the kind of place you make good friends quickly. Doing so much together creates opportunities for your lives to rapidly become entwined. It's an encouraging place and one where you can be more open and vulnerable. I didn't go to university so this was my coming of age experience. Much of what I learned then has stayed with me and continues to shape me.

Mark, Rich, me and Simon – 4 gardeners just chillin'.

Me, Nigel, Nige and Toby, a.k.a. The Banana Brothers.
Cool, aren't we?

The Pox!

As 1987 kicked in good and proper I began to feel ill. A few days before this I had been sitting in the Octagonal lounge at Lee Abbey, effectively the conference room, and heard that further down the row was a little girl who had chickenpox, or was recovering from it or something. Days later I had nausea, the shakes and the first few signs of spots starting to come through. I didn't know what I had but Meg, a member of the community who had previously been in nursing, came into my room, took one look at my arm and went, 'Mm hmm.' In that diagnosing kind of way.

Before long my face was starting to resemble a pizza, and the itches were kicking in. The next thing I knew my parents had turned up and they were bundling me into the car. It's three weeks at home for you my boy. And so it was. The first few days and nights were rough and the spots came out good and proper, but with mum's tender care and the space to relax and forget all the normal pressures, I began to feel like things weren't so bad really. I watched a few movies, I particularly recall *Rocky IV* in the middle of a restless and itchy night when I couldn't sleep. The Italian Stallion and that big blond Dolph Lundgren knocking ten bells out of each other. I had thought they did it to *Eye of the Tiger*, but it turns out that was *Rocky III* staring Mr T. The little grey cells do tend to muddle things up.

One of the books I read during that time really impacted me. *The Flying Scotsman* by Sally Magnusson is a biography of *Chariots of Fire* athlete Eric Liddell. He was a man of great dedication and integrity. He was also very caring and down-to-earth. He went to China after winning his Olympic gold medal and was imprisoned during the war in a Japanese internment camp. Whilst there he put up shelves for a prostitute in her room. She said he was the first man who had done something for her without wanting anything in return.

There is a moment towards the end of Luke's gospel when two people bump into a Messiah in disguise as they're leaving town. Afterwards, as they recall the conversation they talk about their hearts burning inside as he spoke to them. I mention that because as I read Eric Liddell's biography I felt something of that, as if God were stoking a fire in me, stirring faded embers, grabbing my attention. I loved Eric Liddell's approach to others. The way he cared. He loved the Beatitudes, which are all about mercy and peacemaking, and God blessing those who are struggling. I realised that caring for people was a way of bearing fruit for God. I began to think about Jonah, and his 'lockdown' time inside that big fish. It was a time for reflection and change for him. A time to reassess. It seemed as if this sudden change of life might be that for me, thankfully without the stomach acid and fishy aroma.

Shhh!

A few mime artists for you:

- Étienne Decroux
- Marcel Marceau
- Desmond Jones
- David Bowie (yes that one)
- Geoffrey Stevenson
- Danny Scott
- Todd Farley
- Mr Bean
- Ken Wylie
- Er… me

Now admittedly you may not have heard of all that lot so a few extra details. Étienne Decroux sort of invented modern mime. The story goes that he and some mates went away for a while, ran about the house with no clothes on and every so often they would freeze (i.e. stand still, not catch hypothermia) and Decroux would sketch the positions of the bodies.

Decroux started a school and taught, among others, Marcel Marceau and Desmond Jones. I saw Monsieur Marceau on stage in 1984. He was in his 60s and still wowing audiences. I nicked a piece he did about wearing masks and getting a smile stuck on his face while he was falling apart inside. It's hard work but I can probably still rattle out a version of it if mime push came to mime shove. And I know that story about Decroux and his pals running about the house sans pants because Desmond Jones told me and a bunch of other wannabe silent-types in a church hall in Shepherd's Bush. Desmond had his own school in London and taught me for three months in Autumn 1988, and I later taught my very good mate Ken Wylie.

Well, that's an exaggeration really. I got Ken miming along with me and we did loads of experimenting with street mime, robotics, church events and school shows. He was a natural so it was a perfect fit. I was the moody one and he was very patient. Eventually, when I gave up miming, Ken went to Desmond's school as I had done. As mentioned earlier, I had started miming in 1981 because of Geoffrey Stevenson.

Top five one-liners people say when they see you wearing white face paint.

1. 'You look a bit pale, mate.'
2. 'You should take an aspirin.'
3. 'Look at him!'
4. (No comment just wide-eyed staring, a bit of pointing and some kind of guffaw or giggle)
5. (My favourite) 'You should eat more red meat.'

Mime gets a bad press really, conjuring up images of Kenny Everett in a top hat and stripy shirt, or Rowan Atkinson saying, 'I am a mime and my body is my tool!' But it can be really effective and moving. After one show a young woman came up to me and told me she had learnt to hide from words, but that she found she could not stop the mime getting through to her.

That There London

I went to mime school in September 1988, ten days after leaving Lee Abbey. (Having been miming for almost seven years I thought it was time I learnt a new skill ☺.) This idea began in the spring of '88, when I was still at Lee Abbey and wondering what to do next. I met a couple who were leading a drama conference there. I chatted to them about future ideas and without batting an eyelid Pip and Rachel advised me I should go to the mime school they had attended.

So on 7th September I left Lee Abbey and headed for that there London. Oscar Wilde once said, 'When a man is tired of London, he is tired of life.' I think I started to feel weary somewhere around Reading. Nothing against the big city but for four years I'd been surrounded by green trees, green hills and green beans. Now it seemed as if the world was turning grey. It was a bit of a culture shock.

It was a shock to find myself in the metropolis after four years in the sticks. I arrived full of confidence and left with my tail between my legs. Twelve weeks at mime school made me realise how much I didn't know.

And not only externally, but internally too. Lee Abbey had stretched me, kept me busy all day every day, pushing and pulling me in a million new directions. Now I was rattling around in London, going to mime school in the mornings and working in the kitchen of the Lee Abbey London student hostel in the afternoons. I felt like a balloon that had been blown up for four years and then let down a little so that I was left all baggy and saggy. I was rattling around within myself. In Devon I'd had little time to think, there was always some new project, some new drama, some new challenge. Now I was becalmed with too much time to think. All kinds of worries and stresses began to creep into the empty spaces in my head.

Things that I have stressed about in my time:

- Money
- Getting things wrong
- Looking foolish
- Being a misfit
- Making small talk
- Saying the wrong thing
- Trips to the dentist
- Trips to the doctor
- Trips to the optician
- Trips to the cinema (Will we be on time?)
- Trips
- Finding work
- Working hard enough
- Working too hard
- Dogs (Never felt at ease with them, and had a few run-ins when I was a boy)

- Rats (Most rodents really. To misquote Indiana Jones, *'Hamsters, why did it have to be hamsters?'*)
- Cats (pooping on the lawn)
- Persecution (Various Christian books have given me the jitters over the years)
- Being embarrassed
- Things being clean
- Taps being off
- Doors being locked
- This list (Have I said too much?)
- Stressing (I worry about worrying too much)
- Plenty of other things

Somebody once said, 'Don't tell me worrying has no effect, most of the things I worry about never actually happen!' Well that was me really, still is, and many of the stresses that threatened to overtake me back then have continued since those days. I have discovered I am a worrier, although I'm the first to advocate that worry doesn't really achieve much, except to impair our ability to function. Perhaps it's a case of 'I worry therefore I am'. I guess the Bible contains so many encouragements to not worry, because God knows how much we do fret.

It annoys me when we're told by news reporters the latest thing that we should 'be worried about'. Why? We can't achieve anything by doing that and we can't solve everything. I like what Jesus says though, he's very down-to-earth about it. 'Who can add a single day to their existence by worrying?' In other words, it just don't achieve much. But if it drives us to action… well that's something else.

But back to mime school. I walked on the spot a lot, pulled faces, bumped into imaginary walls, picked up a million invisible cups, and learnt how to put on lip stick and eye liner. Halfway through the course, and starting to realise how much I didn't know, I decided I was the worst mime artist in the world. I don't think I was alone in feeling that. I plummeted. One guy I befriended there said to me one day, 'Don't let it get you down.' At least that was the gist of what he said. 🙂 I really appreciated that. Sounds simple but never underestimate the power you have to encourage another human being.

On another occasion, as I walked back to the student hostel I glanced up and locked eyes with a stranger coming the other way. They smiled at me as they passed by. Something about that moment lifted my spirits. One human being taking an interest in another, even fleetingly, can make a difference.

At the end of the three month course we were to perform in a final show for friends and family. I struggled to come up with something till a friend on the course suggested we work together. We did a comedy piece about a weatherwoman becoming increasingly drunk. It went fine in rehearsal but I didn't do well in the performance. I felt a failure. The next morning I led community prayers at the

Lee Abbey student hostel, and people really appreciated it. I felt there was a lesson in this, I often do better when communicating about God than I do when simply trying to entertain. It's a lesson I have to keep on learning.

It was only when I'd left mime school that I realised how much I'd learnt. I've been teaching people to walk on the spot, pull faces, create the universe and get trapped in invisible boxes ever since.

Insight

At various times during my Lee Abbey years I had wondered what I would do next. That's the downside of Lee Abbey for me, it's always temporary. Guests come and go every week, community friends come and go every year, and before you know it you're the one walking round a sad leaving circle saying goodbye. When I pitched up at LA in '84 I came with the idea of going on from there to do a stint with outreach organisation *Youth With a Mission*. However, friends and I started to banter about getting a double-decker bus and touring the country as a theatre company. Thank goodness we didn't. We might well have killed each other! As a result of my driving if nothing else.

When I did eventually leave in '88 I headed off to Desmond's mime school for those three months, and then started working freelance as a solo mime artist. Towards the end of '89 I moved to High Wycombe to share a house with two of my friends from Lee Abbey, Chris and Soobie. Folks I'd bantered with about the double-decker bus. The three of us went along to a conference together and I went down with a bad cold. (Ironic eh – go to a healing conference and get ill!) So I skived the last full day, and as I lolled about in a friend's house, musing on some of what I'd heard in the conference a seed of an idea took root. Why didn't the three of us form a creative community? A theatre company of sorts.

A few weeks earlier Chris and Soobie had been offered a house totally rent free, by a local minister. It was large enough to comfortably house five of us. We contacted other friends from our Lee Abbey days and Boom! *Insight* was born. No double-decker bus mind you. Soobie and Jo were dancers, Julia and I mime artists, Chris sang and played guitar. And we could all act. So that was the next two and a half years sorted.

However, before joining *Insight*, I zipped off to South Africa for seven weeks with my friend Alan, yes the chaplain whose room we turned upside-down. Alan was to be a great facilitator for *Insight* and for my work after. In 1989, across a library table he mentioned his forthcoming trip and asked if I'd like to go. I went. And caught up with lots of South

African friends from those Lee Abbey days. Within 48 hours of landing we were up in the Drakensberg mountains, drinking fresh water from the falls. Later I took the Garden Route down to the Cape. Too much beauty to crowbar into a few words. Enough to say that it was the trip of a lifetime.

After the heat and dazzle of South Africa it was back to reality and a blustery February in England. *Insight* began, we decorated the house, and Chris and I took off in a hired van to pick up some spare furniture from Chris's parents. When I took over the driving disaster struck. I mistakenly pressed the brake when I meant to hit the clutch. We were braking and accelerating at the same time. Not advisable. The wheels locked and we shot off the motorway and up a bank speckled with trees. In my mind's eye I could see a branch piercing the windscreen and penetrating my skull. It didn't happen. The van came to a halt and we leapt out. What to do now? The thing was parked at an acute angle, in danger of toppling at any moment. We ummed and ahhed and eventually one of us suggested praying. Before we'd even said 'Amen', a police car came round the bend and screeched to an abrupt halt. Two gentlemen in blue appeared with the immortal words, 'You can't park that there.' We chatted and eventually they stayed as Chris did his best to reverse the van down to safety. Mercifully there was very little damage. Mostly our nerves and my ego. The return journey was less eventful.

We set up the community home and got on with the next two and a half years of school assemblies, street theatre, church gigs and workshops. We performed in living rooms, in draughty tents and on blustery streets, even on a low-ceilinged barge once. And I vaguely recall one church hall where the local lads were banging on the door as we performed. No doubt desperate to see our world-class show.

From January 1990 to August 1992 we lived, ate, worked, performed, chilled, worshipped, messed about and bantered together. How we laughed! We had a ball. Every day was a total blast! Never a cross word. And if you believe that...

I learned that living in a Christian community of five in urban High Wycombe was light years away from living in a community of 80 on a beautiful estate in Devon. We had some great times together, shared lots of fun and genuine friendship, but we were five different temperaments and personalities. On good days it was enriching and enlightening. On bad days it was enriching and enlightening. Just not in a happy, smiley way.

One of the things I did love about *Insight* was the way we used ordinary stuff to communicate our faith. We performed to songs like *Stand by me*, *Why do fools fall in love* and *Another day in paradise*. We also met together each morning for daily prayers and being a creative bunch we tried all kinds of things. We weren't afraid to experiment with new ideas, and this bled into our work. Many of the lessons from our Lee Abbey days got us through small community living, we knew what it took to meet together regularly, to worship, clean the house, rehearse. Even cook. Well, I say cook. Hmm. The other four were great at it. Let's just leave it at that.

There was a building not far from us called *The Wycombe Six*. Now I know that sounds like a band of hoodlums, but it was in fact our local multiplex. We saw *The Commitments* there, about some friends forming an Irish soul band. We loved it along with a bunch of other films too, like *The Dream Team,* and *Memphis Belle. The Dream Team* gave us one of our best-loved tunes – *Hit the road Jack* was a firm favourite. But I can be a moody git at times (Who'd have thought it, eh?), and living so closely together brought that out. At times I hid away, unable to cope with the close proximity of four other lives.

One defining moment for *Insight* occurred at the North Devon Agricultural Show. We were performing street theatre in white face paint, but in a fenced off area way back from the audience. We were frustrated by our lack of impact. Richard, my gardening boss from Lee Abbey days dropped by and suggested we try throwing our nets over the other side. Hmm. We mulled on this and decided to hop over the fence and start posing as statues right in the middle of those wandering by.

We were nervous about it but it worked and it defined how I would do street theatre for the next six or seven years. Using robotics and statues to grab attention and hand out leaflets about following Jesus. We found that folk were less likely to throw away the leaflets taken if they had chosen to take them from a white-faced mime statue!

I may well have expected our creative community to be a kind of utopia, or perhaps a cross between *The Good Life*, *The Waltons* and *Summer Holiday*. It didn't turn out like that. It wasn't exactly *Withnail & I* either, so much went so right and we clearly saw God's provision and blessing. I had once claimed that *Insight* would last a decade. It didn't. I was restless. I wanted to head off on my own again. I had an idea about offering training courses to church drama groups. So in August 1992 we went our separate ways.

Quiet Man

No, not that old movie with John Wayne. Something else. A couple of words that snuck into my head whilst I was hearing a talk by Michael Mitton on our church weekend. I think this was sometime in 1992 whilst still in *Insight*. We all went on our church weekend together.

Michael referenced the white stones in chapter two of the book of Revelation. Stones that bear a new name from God. He suggested we might want to reflect on this and see if God had a name for us, something positive and uplifting. I didn't even have to reflect. As he was talking two words snuck into my head. *Quiet Man*. This wasn't perhaps what I would have ever thought of myself, but there was both humour and encouragement in that little message. Humour because, well... what is a mime artist if not quiet? And more importantly I am hopeless at small talk and making conversation. This is something that would lead to a crisis in the future. I should have held on more tightly to that name. *Quiet Man*. God knows us well, doesn't he, we often say that. But it's so hard to get that into my thick skull and calloused heart. He understands us better than we understand ourselves. And that day he was trying to help me with my regular, earthy struggles.

Even as I type this now I'm aware how easily I forget this name and put myself down when I can't find the words to relate to others. It seems such hard work at times. Part of life's ongoing stress. Especially if I compare myself to others who seem to find it so easy. But we'll come back to all that.

Quiet Man. I wrote it down in the front of my new pocket New Testament. Which I later dropped in the Gents' loos. Not too close to the urinals thankfully. That's life isn't it? Incredible, uplifting, divine stuff going on, right in the middle of our muddling and bumbling.

I love small Bibles by the way. I'm a sucker for them. If you could buy an inflatable Amplified Bible that you could collapse and carry with you everywhere I'd buy it. Or maybe a holographic one. Ooh... there's a thought.

It's Matrimony (to quote Gilbert O'Sullivan)

It was the year of *Four Weddings and a Funeral* so we invited everyone to *One Wedding and a Reception*. Lynn and I met at Lee Abbey in 1993 and fell for each other while she was filling up her hot water bottle. I'm an old romantic. Actually, it was midnight and she told me and a friend that her *Paddington* hot water bottle was her man substitute. Well, what can I say, she had me as *man substitute.*

I was by then living in Woking, and was working solo again offering drama courses to churches, tearing around the country teaching folks to walk on the spot and get stuck in invisible phone boxes. I had also started working with Ken. Our double-act came about because Ken had been a star pupil on a residential training weekend held by *Insight* in our home church, one of the last events we did together. At the last session, as Ken was walking out of the door he looked back and said, 'Maybe one day we'll appear on the same stage.' His comment stayed with me and when I moved to Woking and needed someone to help me do street theatre there I got on the blower. It was the start of a great friendship.

Did I mention being terrified of commitment? I think I did but I wouldn't want to commit to that… While Lynn and I were *courting* (great word that) a friend of ours took me aside one day.

'This is not a word from God,' he said, 'it's a word from Geoff.' That was his name, by the way. 'Don't lose Lynn. Occasionally you find someone really different in life and Lynn is one of those people.'

I might have a run a mile if he *had* said it was a word from God, but because he was so down-to-earth and gentle in his encouragement I listened. Likewise my vicar Malcolm, who knew me well (the one who had advised me to reapply to Lee Abbey in Weston and had now moved to Woking), asked me if I was going to stick with the relationship this time. Again it was just a gentle question, but something about it sank in. It was the kind of encouragement I needed.

We also needed a house though. And this was the first of many accommodation miracles we have seen over the years. I was busy in Woking while Lynn was miles away in North Devon. She sat down to serve the meal one evening and found herself next to a lady from… Woking. The subject turned to houses and this guest mentioned she was about to head off to theological college. That meant she would have an empty property in Woking. Boom! Thank you Lord.

We married on 1st September on a blustery Thursday at the end of a hot dry summer. It was a perfect day, all the usual things. Friends, family, speeches, nerves, cake, laughter, champagne. The service was led by a host of our Lee Abbey friends, Malcolm married us and Geoff spoke. And afterwards our friends faithfully turned our car into Chitty Chitty Bang Bang. We drove off into the night while the live folk band from the reception played us off. The whole thing felt like a perfect bubble.

Agghh!

I continued doing gigs around the country performing mime and teaching drama, often with Ken, and now Lynn came with me to help out. Not so much performing drama, but she was great at narrating pieces and has a beautiful singing voice. However, the stress levels were starting to rise and I felt like the wheels were showing signs of coming off.

Still, we soldiered on and went with Ken to a gig in Torrington. The town regularly plays host to an event which commemorates the English Civil War, and Ken and I were invited to do some street theatre as a kind of outreach during the event. Great. The town would be chocka with tourists and we happily assumed they would lap it up. So we packed our ghetto-blaster, donned our black outfits and white gloves and made for the West Country.

They didn't lap it up, they were too busy lapping up other stuff elsewhere. As sometimes happens with public events the Christians find themselves performing in a side alley to a dirty puddle and an old brick wall. We did anyway. For me Torrington was a brick wall too far. I had soldiered on now for eight years, doing street mime in Birmingham, London, Reading, Woking… oh and a whole host of other A-Z places. Stomaching the blank expressions and embarrassed passers-by. For years I had watched people walk past me as if I was invisible, some glaring as if I was a walking dog turd, some sneering as if I was just an idiot. I'd had enough. (Can you tell I was angry!?)

Halfway through one of our mimes I tore off my gloves and slapped them theatrically onto our stage mat. It was a sincere performance I can tell you, genuine diva stuff, but no one cared anyway, no one was watching, we were miming to thin air. As far as the masses of Torrington were concerned we were just paint drying. I felt like an angry waste of space, a chaotic fake on legs. I just didn't want to do this anymore.

People don't realise how vulnerable you are when you mime. They don't know that sometimes you feel like a slug on a salt diet. You want to curl up and die. Especially if no one is appreciating the effort you're putting in. Well, I'd curled up and cringed internally once too often. I wasn't going on. Poor Ken was left to entertain the hordes, even if they were elsewhere watching someone cock a musket. The true professional that he is, Ken turned the sketch into a piece of solo robotics, kept going till the backing track finished, then he paused, held the final pose, before coming off to console me.

Something had to give.

Who Wants to Have a Midlife Crisis?

A quiz! Why do some men have a midlife crisis? (N.B. there are no big money prizes on offer here.)

a) Not looking like Brad Pitt or George Clooney
b) Not having a big enough TV
c) Not having enough t-shirts with slogans on
d) Not being able to grow a bushy beard
e) Having a Reliant Robin and not a Tyrannosaurus 4x4
f) Being more Mr Bean than Sean Bean
g) All the shelves we put up keep falling down
h) Never having shot our guns in the air shouting 'Agghh!' (See movies *Point Break* and/or *Hot Fuzz*)
i) Hitting middle age and fearing that our dreams will never ever EVER be fulfilled
j) Reaching the top of the mountain and not liking the view (metaphorically)
k) Looking down at our belly and not liking the view (literally)
l) Not being able to understand the words of the songs in the 'hit parade'
m) Thinking that *The Birdie Song* is not a bad dance number after all

According to Today.com the most likely reasons men have a midlife crash are... a) fear that we'll never achieve our dreams, or b) having achieved them we then don't know what to do next. In other words, the shelves we put up have fallen down, or reaching the top of the mountain we find we don't like the view. Well done if you got it right. Apologies for the lack of big cash prizes.

There are probably many reasons, or at least many versions of these reasons. Nick Page in his book *Dark Night of the Shed* talks about realising that 'this ship is sinking'. Another author Don Miller describes life like a bestseller, and us making the discovery that there are now more pages in your left hand already read than there are in your right still to be devoured.

One of the big problems is we don't know how to articulate what is going on. We're afraid to look weak, and embarrassed to be honest about the things which bother us. I don't know much about CALM (Campaign Against Living Miserably) but it seems to me that any folks who speak up and offer support for us middle-aged lost souls are doing a good thing.

CVM (Christian Vision for Men) are a good lot too. Inspiring guys to grow in their faith and to let Jesus into all the troubles a man can face. We guys are so good at wearing our masks, or our fig leaves. We're past masters at blending in. It's easier and safer that way. Thank God for those who are not afraid to stick their necks out, to call a spade a spade, and to offer to help the rest of us along life's pot-holed, junk-strewn safari.

Crash!

I suppose it began sometime in the mid-'90s, and on the Torrington gig the cracks really started to show. I couldn't hide them anymore. Things really came to a head when we took part in a Lee Abbey church mission weekend. It was Autumn 1996 and I had been working full time in Christian mime and drama for eight years, if you included my time with Lee Abbey that was another four. But it was really the eight years on the road that culminated in the crash. Though it's hard to truly explain what was going on. I had by then been going to church for well over 35 years, and to be honest I had become increasingly bored on Sundays as the services chugged by. I was hungry for something more, but I didn't know what.

And then there was the evangelism thing, and that's really what brought this to a head. In the middle of this church mission I went for a walk. A kind of 'I can't do this' kind of walk. I was being honest with myself. I found it so hard to communicate my faith in conversation with people and I felt a fraud. I had done loads of faith-sharing missions in the past with Lee Abbey, and as a mime artist, but I just couldn't talk the talk. Or talk the walk. And I wasn't that good at walking the talk, so the whole thing was a shambles really. It was no good.

Plus there was the Torrington factor, The gigs that felt like painful failures. The detritus had been building up, and I didn't know what this meant. I felt overwhelmed by disappointment and failure. I wanted someone to give me a break, instead of feeling pressured all the time. This Christianity thing was too hard, too demanding. I was growing more and more stressed about performing mime and drama in public, the thing had become a burden. And now here I was ranting to myself as I wandered aimlessly in a kind of no-man's land on a church mission. Looking for the emergency exit.

Immediate help was at hand. Lynn and I chatted to the lady who was hosting us and she asked if we'd thought of taking some sabbatical time. A breather. We jumped on the idea. It was September '96. We had bookings for a year but could keep a clear diary for Autumn '97. I couldn't wait. Hopefully this would solve everything. Three months out, away from the pressure. Brilliant!

I probably had a few ups and down in the following year but we made it through. I think the disappointments and challenges were a little easier to deal with as I wasn't passionate about the work anymore. It sounds terrible but I had just given up caring. So September '97 came and we stopped.

I felt as if my whole existence was in dire need of a spring clean, a re-tread, a fuel injection, a makeover, an overhaul, a deep clean, a lick of paint, a scrub and brush up, a wash and blow dry, a shot in the arm and any other fresh start clichés you care to mention.

In the summer of '97 we had been to the wedding of a friend, and the groom's mum had suggested I chat with a lady near us who ran a small retreat centre, perhaps she could help. So as the sabbatical kicked in I went. I can't remember our conversation as we sat in the peaceful, sunny garden at that gentle place, a world away from the rush and hustle, but somehow at some point a penny dropped. I wasn't going back to miming.

I got home and told Lynn. It wasn't the best of news without a plan b. But I was convinced. I felt a kind of relief, and was hopeful that another career in writing would open up. Surely it would. God could do anything, so making me rich and famous as an author would be a walk in the park for him. Wouldn't it?

Nimrod's and Housestairs

The thing was this. I had a gift for drama which people appreciated, yet I was finding it increasingly difficult to use it. And that may well have added to the stress of those days. At one time it would have seemed unthinkable to me that I should stop miming, yet as time went by I began to get a sense that if I let the drama stuff fall away and die it would become a kind of manure in the ground, feeding the seeds of something new. I know this sounds a strange analogy but it was definitely an idea hovering in the back of my head. I hung on to it. It provided a glimmer of hope.

When I gave up miming I gave up a lot of things. Direction, purpose, hope, evangelism. I hadn't lost my faith in God, but I had crunched into a wall. I was fed up with myself, the church, and the kind of faith I had been holding on to. So I let go. I went into a kind of spiritual freefall and... well I didn't plummet or go splat into anything... I just kept on falling. The plan to not go back to doing drama was extremely liberating, but also a tad worrying – what else was I going to do? Obvious really, be a famous, successful and rich fiction writer. It was what I'd always wanted to do, so quite clearly God was going to throw wide the doors and make it all happen. Wasn't he?

Turns out not. I contacted publishers, and waited and hoped and watched the post and waited and hoped and watched the post and waited and hoped and watched the post. Nothing. There was a glimmer of hope when one publisher showed an interest in one of my children's adventures *Lucy Housestairs and the Assassins*, but too many months and one rewritten end later... and... nothing. Tumbleweed. I ended up doing three part-time jobs – working as a cinema usherette (scary but inspiring), a garden centre receptionist (nice but I had no idea what I was doing) and a church caretaker (moving furniture, making tea and an interesting experience clearing up a toilet cubicle). I was lost, angry, confused and miserable. But I kept on writing. Inside though, I think I still felt that there was a gulf between what I was able to write and what I was supposed to write.

I had been writing stories for a while. Most of them children's adventures. First there was a quartet of fantastic tales featuring a character called Jimmy Deal and cartoon villain Jordan Badd. Then there was a trilogy about Nimrod's academy for action heroes. And in between the tale I mentioned above – a gung-ho, good natured, shoot-em-up-with-water-pistols adventure that spirals out of control in *Lucy Housestairs and the Assassins*. The one that nearly bagged me a publisher. I loved writing these and now had time to dedicate to developing novels and contacting publishers.

I had also finished a contemporary rewrite of the gospels, that I began in the early '90s, *Still Life*. And a fictional diary that I imagined God might have kept (not presumptuous in any way at all!). Plus a fictional diary of my time at Lee Abbey (which I read again recently and really loved, but it only works if you were actually there at the time). And also *Slow Suicide*, a mystery drawing on my trip to Cambodia. Oh, did I mention that? I went to Cambodia.

The temples at Angkor Wat, in the north of Cambodia. Astonishing remnants of the Khmer Empire which dominated the region for 400 years from about 800AD. I didn't spot Indiana Jones amongst the ruins, but I wouldn't have been surprised if he'd have popped up, fleeing from a fast moving boulder or some rampant rats. 'Rats, why did it have to be rats?'

Radio Radio

By 1999 I had approached more publishers than you could shake a rejection letter at; I'd written quite a few books and yet it had all come to nothing. Well, not quite nothing. Kevin Mayhew publishers were interested in our Frisk and Dexter interactive Bible adventure. I had read a couple of books as a boy where you could decide which page to turn to next. Lynn and I concocted a similarly interactive biblical yarn featuring Tintin style time-travelling duo Frisk and Dexter. Kevin Mayhew were keen to take it on.

Frisk and Dexter ran a time travel investigation agency. They were detectives who could investigate any crime from any time. They had a large brown office, with brown files and brown furniture and brown windows and brown swivel chairs. When the purple phone on Dexter's brown desk rang like an old school bell, they knew that a case from history was calling them. All they had to do was pick up the phone and they'd travel back through time to the scene of the case.

Around this time I bit the bullet and took a job working in our local six-screen cinema. It would be the first of those three part-time jobs I took on in the next 18 months. We needed the money.

I began to wonder about Moses, the Egyptian-killing prince who had to flee for his life. He ended up in the wilderness looking after sheep and I found myself wondering if he looked back on his prince of Egypt days and thought – is that it? Are my glory days done now? Did he imagine looking after sheep for the rest of his days? (He was of course in training in that desert but didn't know it.) I began to wonder if we'd be struggling for the rest of time now. I was losing hope and couldn't see a way forward.

Then one evening I went with our minister, Malcolm, to take part in a local radio broadcast, and that's where I met Steve. Steve presented a regular weekly God slot and he seemed quite interested in me. As he walked across the station floor towards me I could sense he was sort of scrutinising me. In a good way though. Suddenly there was a small flicker of light. Would I come along and regularly present a film slot on his evening programme? The idea really appealed, I loved films and was now seeing new ones regularly in my cinema job.

So that became a part of my week. Reviewing films I had seen in my cinema job. And along the way I also helped edit a video for Steve's organisation *Soapbox*. I had never edited video before, but it would turn out to be prophetic.

It was Steve who invited me to go with him to Cambodia, and a year later to Kenya. Both experiences opened my eyes and my heart to the wider world. The impact still courses through my veins really. Especially from the trip to Cambodia. We met some fantastic people who had lived through incredibly tough times. We visited a micro business, where very poor families were able to make a living and start saving for the kind of things we take for granted over here. I met others my own age who had lived through the horrors of Pol Pot and the murderous Khmer Rouge. Their stories were deeply disturbing. One woman had lost 14 members of her family. Unimaginable.

We went to the Killing Fields, where countless people had been executed and their bodies concealed in massive pits in the ground. And to Tuol Sleng, the torture centre, formerly a high school. I found that the most distressing, so terrible to think of the horrors perpetrated there. I cut short my time on the tour of the buildings and had to go outside. I stood there, wrestling with the emotions inside, staring at the same piece of ground where so much pain had been inflicted and blood spilled. More than 20,000 people had suffered here.

Later we went to Angkor, the city of ancient temples in the northern jungles of Siem Reap. A jaw-dropping ancient complex which really did look like something out of an Indiana Jones movie. 1000 years old, mystical and thrilling, I would later revisit this experience in a modern gospel, *Sons of Thunder*.

Popcorn

Kids really know how to decorate a cinema carpet with popcorn. It's as if they place the bucket carefully on the floor, then kick it with such skill and finesse that the yellow puffs of corn spread out like a huge fan. A sticky golden mosaic just lying there, waiting for someone like me to come along and sweep it up when the show's over.

I struggled to fit in at the cinema, though I did love seeing so many films. With hindsight I can say that, like Moses in the desert, I was in training and didn't know it. I had no idea at the time though and the problem was I was twice the age of most of the others working there. At the end of an evening they would pile into a car, drive a couple of hours and go clubbing. I would limp home to Horlicks and bed. Actually that's not true, I just went to sleep. After my first shift I was so exhausted I crawled into bed and fell asleep with my contact lenses still in. On the shifts I kept my head down, tried not to do anything embarrassing and didn't mention my faith. My confidence was at an all-time low. However, half of the building was given over to a theatre and I found I fitted in a little better when I did shifts with the theatre guys. So as much as I loved the movies I signed up for a good number of theatre shows too.

And in the background I wrote, reviewed films for Steve and wondered where it was all going. Things kind of came to a head when we attended a weekly Sunday evening course at church. On evangelism. After the last class I kind of flipped, proclaiming it all to be bollards. Out loud. Except I didn't say *bollards*. I don't think I upset anyone, just myself. But I couldn't take it anymore. I was tired of the demands that Christianity seemed to make on me. I couldn't do that stuff. I couldn't be a 'contagious Christian' as the course was asking me to be. The only things other folks were likely to catch from me was dissent, apathy and cynicism. Not really the kind of things that spark a revival.

Church meant little to me. Though I appreciated the wisdom and friendship of our minister Malcolm. He felt that we needed to step out of the traffic, take some time to refurbish our spiritual life. He suggested we write down all the dreams and big ideas and hopes that had come to nothing and set fire to them. We did. I kept the ashes for a while. It was as if all we had hoped for had become like weights pulling us down. We had been nurturing various ideas and dreams in the previous couple of years. Lynn is an artist and we had dabbled in a card making idea we called *Blue Box*. Malcolm said one more thing too, that God was taking us into exile. Oh great. And he wanted us to settle there for a while. Yikes. There's a bit in Jeremiah chapter 29 where the people are stuck in exile and the prophet tells them to settle and make homes there. That was the gist of it.

We also prayed with a couple of friends in our church, and just as we were leaving them the husband happened to mention a couple of verses from the book of Haggai. It was only a passing comment. And yet it wasn't. It was a bombshell, and I quote:

You plant much but you harvest little.
You have scarcely enough to eat or drink…
Your income disappears as though you were putting it into pockets full of holes.
You hope for much but get so little…
Haggai 1 v 6

You can say all that again! I went straight home and read this passage and boy! did it hit the spot. All our disappointments right there. It seemed to symbolically sum them up. Suddenly everything seemed to have a negative slant. I had wanted to change the world but the world wouldn't play ball. In the bank I did my best to convert everyone and (how dare they) they wouldn't comply. I had wanted to transform Weston-Super-Mare back in those enthusiastic new Christian, drama group days but Weston wasn't for turning.

In *Insight* I had endeavoured to build a community that would last a decade and spread its influence far and wide, in the end we dispersed after two and a half years. I had paced the streets of this country, gleaming white face and smart bright gloves on, miming to happy tunes, and people had just ignored me, as if I was a pile of horse dung they needed to skirt round. I had hoped for so much and got so little. The verses from Haggai smacked me between the eyes. Okay we had food in the fridge and a roof over our heads, but the finances were depleting and the well was running dry.

I began to compile a book of scribblings, expressions of what I was feeling. I called it *Nightmare on Evangelical Street*. It's full of thoughts and notes from the time. Including a lovely letter from my parents encouraging me to keep going and… 'who knows in future years you may find yourself telling others to do the same.' Here's one of the pieces from it.

Unknown Territory

It is hard to obey.
Hard to hand over the goods.
Somehow I always end up struggling to obey at every little decision.
Instead of just giving you the lot and having done with it.

I want to get every last word right.
Every turn, every move, every breath.
But I can't, God really knows I can't.
I'm tired.
Exhausted from not letting go.

God please cut me loose and let me fall into the unknown country that lies in the palm of your hand.
It looks dark in there, it looks fearsome and painful.
But there's a chance that it may not be.
Others have been there and reported otherwise.
Will I ever trust their telling?

A Bear with a Bow and Arrow

Another bit of the Bible that grabbed me was Lamentations chapter three. It's an extraordinary passage about how the author (Jeremiah?) is attacked on his way home by a bear that grabs him, fires painful arrows into him, gives him something nasty to drink, hurls him to the ground and knocks six bells out of him. He then finishes up by grinding his teeth in the dirt.

At least, this is how Jeremiah feels. There may well have not been a vicious multitalented bear at all. This is Jeremiah's way of describing how he feels life has ambushed him. Taken away his purpose and joy. This tale grabbed me for two reasons. Firstly it's jolly honest to say that's how you feel about things, not trying to dress up your frustration and pain just because you believe in God. But secondly, and most importantly, Jeremiah goes on to recite a couple of verses I knew well. 'In spite of this mess,' he says, 'God's mercies are new every morning, God's love never ends, great is his faithfulness.'

He's able to hold in tension the notion that God is good and life is hard. And I think he's saying something about needing to find God in the small things, because the big things have all gone wrong. In a sunrise, in a smile, in an act of kindness. He says too, that he'll never forget the terror of this time, yet he'll still dare to hope in God.

Wolves and Bushes

Frisk and Dexter and the drama books I had written had not kept the wolf from the door. So we did our best to make friends with the wolf. Adjust to the pressures and predators. But we were running out of money, optimism and ideas.

And then unexpectedly, in our wilderness, a bush burned. Though we didn't know it at the time. We heard that a cottage in the little village where Lynn's parents lived was up for rent. We laughed about the idea but did nothing. A couple of months later it was still up for rent. We came back from a very wet trek around town to find a hefty leak in our lounge. It felt somehow like the last straw, I mean, our video collection was soaked for goodness sake! This was serious. 😊 It certainly seemed like a nudge of some kind.

We upped and went. Fled the South-East. Did up the cottage for two months whilst living with Lynn's parents. I laid floor tiles, rollered ceilings and varnished curtain rings. There was something cathartic about all that painting and sanding and grouting. Plus the setting was idyllic. Standing in the small field at the back of the cottage, strimming grass, I was transported back to my days working in the gardens at Lee Abbey. Could there be some hope? I wasn't sure. Would anything ever work out?

Lynn had booked to do a listening course at Lee Abbey and I trailed along with her. Lee Abbey was always the perfect place to escape. While she attended the sessions I hid in the library and read old books. I had started revisiting classics from the past, anything that might inspire me again. I had already re-read *Run Baby Run* and now picked up a copy of a book by Colin Urquhart. *My Father is the Gardener*, a fictional account of God reviving a sleepy, traditional church. I was desperate to try and rekindle some meaning, some purpose from the past. For light relief I re-read *Stig of the Dump*. Neither book promised any light for the end of the tunnel, but revisiting these old reads was heartening and distracting.

Then we had a chat with a couple of old friends who were working on the community at Lee Abbey. Had we considered going back as summer workers? No. Not at all. But now you mention it…

I don't remember the process but it was quickly agreed upon. We would return for three weeks in July and help out as part of the community.

Then Lynn got pregnant.

Amy

We had been trying for a baby for a few years. But nothing had happened. Now, having left Woking and moved to the sticks, boom! Or bam! Or whatever you want to say. We were going to have a baby. And be summer workers at Lee Abbey. Things were starting to change fast. We laid out a babygrow on our bed and imagined a small person in it. Yikes. Wow. My goodness. I was going to be a dad. Me! A dad. Me! ME!

We discovered Lynn was pregnant not long before our planned trip back to Lee Abbey, and by the time we came to pack our bags she was looking decidedly green. Lynn was having very bad all-day sickness. She was not going to be up to it. So I went alone and Lynn moved back in with her parents.

It was strange being back. Community life there had changed in some ways, plus 13 years had passed and I was no longer a young gun full of confidence. I *was* full of questions though and it gave me a chance to talk about some of these. The environment at Lee Abbey is an incredibly encouraging one. And that lifted my spirits. I even ended up doing a couple of mimes again. On my first day off I spent a precious morning sitting in the sun on the front lawn, overlooking the bay. It was an idyllic spot, and a million miles from the muddle of my normal life. I sat there in a peaceful bubble, reading a letter I'd received from my old school friend Jonathan from Cornwall. (From those Ellery Queen and Redruth Grammar days.) Nothing had been resolved and I was only here for a few weeks. Little more than a gasp for air really. But sitting on the grass, soaking up that ageless view, it was enough to imagine for those moments that all was well with the world.

That said, I felt a kind of malaise, a lack of connection with things. I felt inadequate too, weak, somehow not enough. I was also surrounded by community members who were decades younger than me. I wanted to travel back in time, I wanted those years back, and couldn't have them. I wanted to feel alive again, vibrant, able to conquer the world. And I wanted a shiny happy faith. I would watch other community members joyfully singing worship songs and wonder if I would ever get back to that kind of exuberance. The reality was different though. I was heading somewhere else.

Three Years!

That first three week stint came to an end and I headed home. But we had already planned another fortnight stint. I couldn't wait to get back. And something else had changed too. Before going back to Lee Abbey I longed for a career in writing from home, but I was aware that contact with others had helped energise me. Perhaps sitting at home punching a keyboard all the time was not the only thing to aim for. We went to Lee Abbey three more times that year. Two weeks, then three weeks, then two weeks. And by the time we had done our last short stint we had been offered a contract to return for longer. For three years. Three years!! Days of stability and friendship, a job and income.

Most folk who work at Lee Abbey go there with a sense of call to community. I have to be honest and say we went because we needed a job. But I'm sure God was in that. Because I was passionate about the ministry of Lee Abbey towards its regular guests. The calling instilled in me back in the '80s was still there. I knew there was value and purpose and inspiration in serving the paying guests who came and went each week. I was up for that if nothing else. And it would be something I would bash on about to other community members for the next nine years.

That's not to say my troubles were over, far from it.

Dad Land

Our gorgeous Amy was born six weeks after we moved to Lee Abbey. The most extraordinary day. I was a father! With a beautiful baby girl! I remember running out of the hospital to get a babygrow from the car (we had forgotten to take it in before the birth) when I spotted a couple of strangers sitting in a car chatting. I ran up to them, banged on the window and shouted, 'I've just had a daughter!' I was so full of life and joy and wonder, I didn't care if anyone thought I was mad or sane. I just wanted to announce it to the world. I wish sometimes that I had that same verve and courage about other things.

Lynn's labour had lasted 36 hours, and it had not been straightforward, going through two epidurals and three midwives. In the next weeks we embarked on that steep learning curve, the one they can't really prepare you for – nappies, colic, sleepless nights, all your routines suddenly in chaos. It shook me up. There were of course plenty of incredible, wondrous, precious moments too. But I had had 39 years of not being a dad, and this learning curve was certainly a steep one.

Amy's first appearance on stage (sadly I don't have a photo) came very early on. A friend and I did a sketch in a Sunday service based on the tale about Solomon settling an argument between two mothers who both lay claim to the same baby. Amy played the tiny baby, being as she was a tiny baby, Mark and I played the two fathers who both claimed her as our own. Solomon then decrees a simple solution. Divide the baby in two. Have half each. A huge rusty saw was brought in (to the gasps of the congregation) and a heated debate followed about which way to split the baby. I can't recall the details so let's just say I played the real dad who immediately gives up any claim to the child, not wanting any harm to come to her. Solomon hands me the baby, realising full well that I am the loving father. It wouldn't be Amy's last time performing at Lee Abbey by any stretch, but it was definitely the first and one of the most dramatic.

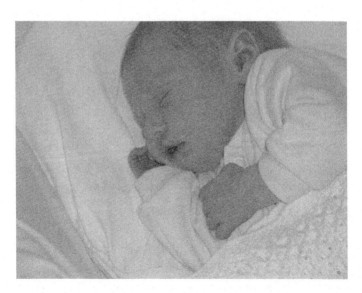

Rollercoasters

Early in 2003 I read Philip Yancey's *Disappointment with God*. I read part of it on a train journey coming back from a trip to the London Lee Abbey student hostel, and I remember my heart burning inside, not unlike the stirring I had felt when reading the Eric Liddell biography back in '87. It felt as if God were starting something, though I had no idea exactly what. Yancey had written the book after a student he knew lost his faith. His publishers had apparently wanted to give it a positive spin, calling it *Overcoming Disappointment with God*, but Yancey refused. This was a book addressing hard questions – why God is invisible, silent, and seemingly unjust.

Yancey revisited the Old Testament and gave me a whole new take on God's interaction with people. The Israelites had crossed the desert with a God they could see (a pillar of fire) and who gave them miracles every day (manna from heaven) yet when they reached the verge of the promised land they did not have a mature relationship with him. Daily interaction with God had not nurtured deep faith and trust. Folk required another way. There was something about Yancey's real and bold take on things that warmed my heart. He described a God who adjusted as things went on, a God who saw how people reacted and worked with that. A God who is interested in how we will respond to life's plateaus and rollercoasters.

Scared and Lost

However, I continued to struggle. I was scared. Scared of being boring. Of being old and dull. Of being trapped. I didn't know what to do. Alongside this Lee Abbey energised me, gave me so many opportunities to try things, experiment, develop new creative ideas. Digital cameras were all the rage and there were no end of beautiful pictures to be taken on the estate. Then one day I got an idea to set the pictures to music with biblical text. I made three of these and we used them in our worship times.

One guest, John, a friend from years past, asked me to make a presentation of images to accompany a U2 song. I did that and he asked me to do another. A friend on the community, Tim, saw the results and asked me to create a visual presentation advertising the proposed new Lee Abbey youth centre. I set to work on that. I had returned to Lee Abbey with the brief of being a creative catalyst, to help other folks develop creative resources and ideas. I had not imagined things going in this direction. Maybe this was a new thing that could solve my troubles.

I was still writing, directing and performing drama, but this carried less stress as people were not coming to see me do my stuff, they were at Lee Abbey for a break or a conference. Anything I offered was simply a bonus. This lifted a lot of the burden from my shoulders. Plus this was not so much about evangelism as helping those who were either Christians or on the fringes of faith. I found I could cope much better with that.

Guests started to see my visual presentations and tell me about other tools available. Other bits of software for editing video. Those days making the *Soapbox* video for Steve may not have been a one-off after all. In 1999 I had also cut together a video of short clips for my minister Malcolm for a New Year's Eve event. Back then I had used two VCRs plumbed together, and a lot of old VHS videos. I'd had no idea back in Woking that these opportunities might turn out to be a prelude to the kind of work I was now starting to do. Who'd have thought? (Well, God for one I guess. ☺)

And then Tim gave me another idea. I loved films, why not use them as a means of talking about life and faith. I jumped at the idea. Not long after returning to work at Lee Abbey I had spotted a book for sale there called *Praying the Movies*. The cover featured a still from one of my all-time favourite films, *Empire of the Sun*. So I bought it. In it Edward McNulty describes scenes from films and relates them to life and faith. I'd never come across this approach before, but started to use it for a kind of daily reflection.

There had been times in the past when I had seen clips from films and thought they'd make useful sermon illustrations, well here was my chance. Perhaps all those hours spent in Woking cinema had not been for nothing. All those big screen films I'd watched, all those people I'd seen coming to be inspired and entertained. Perhaps, like Moses, I had been in training for something and didn't know it.

Inspired by Tim's suggestion and Edward McNulty's book I started doing regular workshops. And people came. I found that movies dealt with all aspects of life and this freed me to talk about my own struggles. It struck a chord. Other folks obviously appreciated this, I wasn't alone with my frustrations and questions.

But I was still scared and feeling lost. I turned 40 as we neared the end of our first year. I started drinking regularly. Spiralling downwards. I was trying to escape. Attempting to be someone other than myself. Because I felt I wasn't enough. So I drank more. And of course it solved no problems. Only added to them. In spite of this good things did continue to happen. I wanted to run away from all my mess. But as they say in therapy, wherever you go, there *you* are. You take yourself with you. Yet, though I wanted to give up on myself, I got the sense that God didn't. He wouldn't let go. And the opportunities continued to open up at Lee Abbey. This was the stark contradiction. I was angry and frustrated and fed up in a place of great beauty, hope and encouragement.

I railed against church too, ranted about how boring and predictable it all was, even talked about how feminised things were on a Sunday morning. One week, when thinking about the church as family, the Sister Sledge track *We are family* was played. It was a great idea for a family service, perfect for the theme, lots of fun and really upbeat, but the next line of that song is 'I've got all my sisters with me!' No wonder, I thought, that real men don't want to go to church. I came out and scribbled down some thoughts, noting that we could have used *Kings of the Wild Frontier* by Adam and the Ants. 'A new royal family, a wild nobility, we are the family!' Now that's more like it.

And yet, when I complained to a friend about how safe everything was and he suggested I go down to the beach one night and sleep in a cave – I was horrified! I didn't want to do that at all. So I was confused. Conflicted. I wanted faith to be more *manly*, but not *manly* in quite that way! I didn't mean I wanted to do more *manly* things.

Tim offered to take a friend and I thrutching, which involves lassoing a rope around yourself and a tree and then climbing up it by thrusting yourself up the trunk. I was terrible at it. It was like being back in the scouts. I felt intimidated. Unable to cope with those kind of physical challenges. Clearly this sort of stuff wasn't the answer. But what was? What *did* I want?

Justin

One thing I *needed* was a good friend. Enter Justin. Thank God for Justin. Someone to stick by me, to laugh at me, listen to me, to offer me a good old fashioned shoulder. It was Justin who tried thrutching with me. (And was much better at it that I was.) One night, with Lynn's help, we both dyed our hair blonde. The next morning a lot of people laughed at us. But in a good, brightening-their-day kind of way. (I'm still dyeing it all these years later.) We went to Spain together in the summer. Lynn suggested he and I go on a jaunt. So we jumped on a plane and just messed about for three days.

On the first evening we walked across a town square in Madrid and Justin tried his Spanish on a couple of local women. They smiled and one said, 'You won't get far with an accent like that, mate!' The two *locals* were from London I think. We travelled a bit, saw some sights, even ended up doing some robotics in a park in Madrid when we met up with three ex-Lee Abbey Spanish friends. We had brought the wooden Lee Abbey logo with us so we could take photos of it in weird places. At one point, while visiting an art gallery, we left it on a bench and I'm sure one or two folk thought it was an obscure and impressive exhibit.

I bought a notebook, and on the final evening in the youth hostel I couldn't sleep, so I wandered into the communal area and started scribbling. Ideas. Thoughts. Random stuff. I don't remember exactly what. But it seems significant looking back.

Above are a few snaps from the trip. Look closely in the top right and you'll spot the Lee Abbey logo on fine display in the art gallery. Middle right our Spanish friends, Sara, Nacho and Maleni can't believe we snuck the logo out of the UK and brought it all the way to Madrid. Bottom right you can see Justin and I scaring the locals with a spot of robotics. Bottom left, Justin climbs a traffic light and tries to put the logo on top. However a few seconds after I took this photo a police car rocked up and we had to run for it!

I can't underestimate the friendship Justin gave me in this time. He was always supportive, always encouraging. On the flight out to Madrid I mentioned that I might just have to accept I'd never be a writer, to which he immediately told me I couldn't say that.

The likely lads. A selfie in the days before selfies.
Note that Justin is smiling and I've brought a frown.

My Way

One of the things that featured highly in my crisis was taking myself too seriously. I discovered I had a great flare for it, I could do it so well. I was the centre of the universe after all. So obviously the cosmos should shift just for me, fall in line with all my demands. Move heaven and earth and Mars (the chocolate and the planet) and Pluto (the dog and the planet) just for me. I was learning of course the meaning of one of the great sayings... the world doesn't owe you a living. I may have thought I was the best thing since sliced bread, but no one else was contract bound to agree with me on that. I wanted to do things my way. (But I didn't have the voice of Sinatra.)

Top Films About Wanting to Rebel
About a Boy (a thirty-something won't grow up)
About Schmidt (a retired guy takes to the road)
Up In The Air (a single guy lives as he pleases)
The Beach (a young guy goes looking for paradise)
Sing Street (a bullied teen falls in love and also forms a band)

I saw *About a Boy* whilst stuck in the raging worst period of things. Will (Hugh Grant) demands that he be able to live like an island, insular, self-sufficient, cut adrift from everyone else, no distracting commitments. I hankered after that. In spite of John Donne's comment (No man is an island etc.) Will proclaims that he *can* be an island, a fun island, a party island, Ibiza. That's what I wanted. To throw off all these shackles and burdens and start really living. Though I had no idea what that really meant.

The Beach is about prodigals, looking for life and adventure, and discovering that, however far you travel, you take yourself with you. I love the book too.

Sing Street is more recent, and a new favourite of mine. It's about a group of teenagers in Dublin in the 1980s. Conor has to move to a tough school and immediately feels all at sea. Then two things happen. He meets a friend, Darren, who tells him he needs a project, a distraction from the daily difficulties. And he sees Raphina, a young woman who tells him she is going to be a model. Conor tells Raphina he needs her to be in a video for a song he's recording with his band. Now he has his project. Because there is no band, no video and no song. But he is in love. So he'll make it happen.

It's a great film about breaking out, dreams, being whole-hearted and succeeding against the odds. My favourite quote occurs after Raphina throws herself into the sea for the video they are making, even though she can't swim. 'Whatever you do, do it with all your heart,' she tells Conor when he pulls her out.

Malaga

And what of Lynn through all this? Well she was extraordinary. So supportive and patient and caring through my selfish, mad times. Continuing to love and support me through all of the chaos, and praying loads for me too, whilst also looking after Amy. I continued to lead houseparties and organise events and do creative activities, whilst having mood swings and tantrums and running around trying to pretend I was still a flippant 16-year-old.

The following spring of 2004, we went to Malaga as a family with Lynn's sister and a few of her friends, and when the weather proved relentlessly grim I

went onto the roof of our villa, sat hunched in my

coat and attempted the makings of a thriller about a guy escaping to Malaga.

The holiday was not easy for many reasons, not least my inability to communicate with the others in the group. I felt insular, odd and inadequate. But the poor weather pushed me to start writing again, drawing on and reimagining my own experiences. I created a character and put him in extreme and dangerous circumstances, it was fiction yet it was also another way of expressing my own problems and insecurities. Years later I put the book on Amazon. It has yet to sell a million. 😊

Amy with two carnations which cost us a 100 euros!
My wallet was deftly picked as I opened it to get a couple
of coins. I was incensed when I discovered it later, yet I
had to admire the flower-seller's dexterity!

Real Men

I continued doing film workshops with the guests and now added another option. *Real Men Don't Go To Church*. The title was deliberately provocative. I wanted guys who felt adrift to feel they weren't alone. And for those of us who faithfully went every week I wanted to ask whether we felt able to take our real selves along on a Sunday. Or a pale imitation. I spoke about the struggles I was having, asked some of the difficult questions out loud. I came across a good number of kindred spirits.

In September 2004 I went to the wedding of my old school friend Jonathan. I stayed on afterwards to house sit while he was on honeymoon and to look after his two sons. When I got back an idea began to develop in my head. What if a disgruntled guy picked up his Bible one night and read the whole thing through, relating it along the way to cultural stuff on the TV and radio. I started typing *The All Night Bible*. It was a preposterous idea of course. Who could ever read a Bible in a single night? But I enjoyed rambling away, playing with ideas, and getting the struggles and questions down on paper. Or at least on a laptop screen.

And then, not long after I started this, Ali dropped in on one of my film sessions. She was an editor for Authentic Media and after my slot she asked if I'd thought of writing anything. I told her about *The*

One Night Bible. She asked me to send her something. It wasn't anywhere near finished of course but I emailed part of it. She came back with some comments. Now the next part is a bit of a blur. Perhaps because of Ali's feedback I started again. This time I had the guy making regular visits to his local pub, drinking Guinness, and reading his leather-bound pocket Bible.

I rewrote various passages of the Bible, stories that appealed to me in my chaotic state, sex, violence, adventure. I contemporised them, made them as readable and fast-paced as I could. Then I had the guy in the pub reflecting on them in a blokey fashion. I'd been reading the likes of Nick Hornby and Tony Parsons for a few years, and had wondered if it were possible to write about the faith in their style. Well, this was my stab at it.

Ali loved it. I remember a phone conversation with her, in which she commented on my writing in a really encouraging way. I was blown away by her enthusiasm for it. I thanked God with all my mixed up heart. It was finally happening!! This was going to print. All we needed was a title. I recall Lynn and I chatting about that, but can't remember who came up with *The Bloke's Bible*. One of us no doubt did, and it stuck.

Vomiting

I still have plenty of mad moments regarding life and faith but I'm learning that we're all a bit bonkers really. And sometimes the mad moments lead to really sane ones. The ongoing crisis (and in 2004/2005 it was still ongoing) was leading me to be a lot more realistic and brutal about my faith in Jesus. And to talk about the mad moments we all have.

So *The Bloke's Bible* was basically me vomiting my frustration and anger and struggles across the page – hopefully in a humorous way. I wasn't sure if anyone would buy it or find it useful. Perhaps it would fast track to the bargain bins. 99p for two!

Not so, it turned out that many folks valued the honesty and humour. I wasn't giving answers, it wasn't another how-to-be-a-really-good-Christian book. If anything it was about how I was finding life stressful, frustrating and overwhelming. But I was also writing about the wayward and reckless Bible guys. I was discovering that the Good Book is full of bad people! Or if not bad then dysfunctional, mid-life crisis types. Brilliant! Seems that the shiny happy people have left the building, and, to quote the great Frederick Buechner, 'God makes his saints out of fools and sinners because there is nothing much else to make them out of.'

My relationship with God was morphing, little by little, as I began to discover a new gritty reality. There were moments in my darkest times when I had sensed that God was still there, against the odds, in spite of my rebellion. This was nothing to do with me and my bad behaviour and everything to do with his refusal to give up on me.

The Bloke's Bible marked a major turning point for me. It was as if I'd finally found something different to say, and my own way of saying it. Years before, in the late '90s, I had visited Adrian Plass with my list of questions about writing, and one of his helpful comments was that I needed to find something different. Well, this was it. I'd found something to say, and something that might just help others too. Writing it had not been hard really, the book tumbled out, a volcanic explosion from my head onto the page. Brutal, raw, as honest as I dared, and hopefully funny.

In the wilderness years, back in Woking, I had done a Christian questionnaire to find my strengths and hopefully an answer to all my woes. The results? My passion was the Bible and my gifting creative communication. The media-based sessions I was now doing and *The Bloke's Bible* both seemed to tap into that. But in a way I could never have foreseen in Woking.

Daylight

In 1999 I wrote a version of this book called *Daylight and Fresh Air*, but as I neared the end I hit a wall. I didn't know how to finish it. I wanted to say that I had broken through the crisis, I was moving into some daylight and fresh air. I wanted to resolve the struggles and anger and disappointment. I wanted to say it was all okay now. But it wasn't. I was still very much in freefall. I hadn't yet found a way forward, I didn't know if I ever would. I may well have been hoping that writing that book would be the answer, but of course it wasn't. It just led me to the same place. Knowing what I had to throw off, but having no idea what I should then pick up. I still have a copy of *Daylight and Fresh Air*, I've been referring to it as I work on this.

Now, in 2004/2005, as I started on the first tiny steps towards hope I began to see the Bible in a new light, and little by little to begin to get to know Jesus all over again. I started to sense his presence with me throughout the day, in the ordinary things, and it bugged me when I went to church and felt that the leaders were grabbing him, pulling him up the front and dictating how we should worship him. I was still angry about lots of things and this was one of them. I found it hard to connect this new burgeoning relationship with Sunday church. It annoyed me too when I heard my friend referred to as Christ. To me he was Jesus, a three-dimensional, caring person.

Balaclavas and Combat Gear

As part of my job as Creative Arts Director at Lee Abbey I wrote three big shows a year. I loved doing Easter, because we always performed the story outside, and involved the guests in the telling of it.

For a few years we did it in period costume, but as time went by I decided to update it and do it in modern dress. I felt it made it more immediate, removed it from simply being a period piece, plus the Roman soldier costumes were not great. Whereas balaclavas, combat gear and replica guns were truly intimidating. Then I heard about a film based on the life of Bob Dylan *I was never really here*. In that move six different actors play Dylan at various ages, and one of them is a woman. Cate Blanchett. And suddenly I saw an opportunity. What if we had four different actors playing Jesus throughout the three days of drama? One on

Thursday evening, two on Friday, and a fourth on Sunday. That meant at least two things. When we performed the resurrection story no one would know who was playing Jesus and so we we were able to have him present and unrecognised through the drama as the narrator, and only reveal his identity at the end! Just like Mary meeting Jesus and thinking he was the gardener. But it meant something else too. It meant we could have a woman playing Jesus. The third Jesus, when our saviour was presented to the crowd, beaten and bloody and completely vulnerable. I felt that this was the moment because when Jesus was arrested and beaten it all looked wrong. When he was taken away and murdered like a criminal, it all looked wrong. So how much more would it look that way in

our drama if Claire appeared as a wounded Jesus when Pilate asked the crowd what he should do.

This is always my intention. Using drama, mime, stories, clips, cultural references… to bring the Bible off the page and into our lives. Never just as a gimmick or as a novelty. Jesus's parables were not the warm-up jokes for his sermons. They were not the light entertainment before the main show. They *were* the message. Creativity that plunged the crowds into the kingdom. And that didn't mean they were always serious. They packed a punch but often used comedy to do so. People laughed, their jaws dropping no doubt at times at the shocks. Then they discussed the surprises and twists, and never forgot them. Gravity and comedy. Hitting home.

I'm so grateful to have these precious reminders of these experiences. The Easter pictures here were taken by the late Barry Renwick, a regular visitor and very good friend

Good Things That Came from the Crash

Admittedly these emerged over time and the line between messy and sorted continues to be a blurred one.

- I became more earthy and realistic
- I realise that failure is an option for us all
- The discovery that God is not afraid of the dark
- I have a desire to be more honest
- Plus an intention to avoid Christian lingo and to use ordinary, regular stuff when trying to communicate about faith and hope

There are plenty of other unspoken things that I'm still processing. And my courage to be more honest and real fluctuates. What I have discovered is that people appreciate reality mixed with faith.

Around 2004 I read a copy of *Messy Spirituality* my Mike Yaconelli. It was gold dust. Stories of real Christianity. People struggling and being honest about that. Mike described himself as the pastor of the slowest growing church in America, because his was a home for misfits and the wounded. I began to share some of the stories in the hope of encouraging others whose lives were messy too. I'm a big fan of Thomas in the gospels, not so much doubting as outspoken about his desires and difficulties.

Chit-Chat

The leaders at Lee Abbey for most of our second stint were Chris and Susan Edmondson. They are such a down-to-earth couple, and I will always be grateful for their encouragement and hands-off approach. They gave me room to experiment and coped with my reckless ideas. They let me dub myself the Loose Canon (!) and let me make mistakes as I tried new things and learned by doing. Susan was my line manager and the perfect person to drop by for occasional chats without seeming heavy-handed in any way. Being the wayward maverick I am I sometimes don't do well with being told what to do. (Hence that episode at the bank when I scribbled *Bank raid loot* on my paying-in slip.)

I began to front chat shows, an hour's evening slot where the guests were... well... *the guests*. I'd show entertaining video clips which would spark conversations amongst those in the audience, and I'd then roam around with a mic asking for comments, opinions and chit-chat on these various subjects. Things like favourite foods, songs, places etc. YouTube was starting to flourish and there was plenty of great material for helping people laugh, relax and discuss a given subject. Also I'd throw in *Room 101*. You know, that place where you can put something and you never have to worry about seeing it again. So on that subject...

My Room 101 Nominations

- High-fiving (it's fine for the High-fiver, but often looks awkward for the High-fivee, especially if it's me)
- Using the car horn in the wrong way (it's there to warn of impending danger, not for telling off other drivers when they make mistakes)
- The words *Awesome* and *Legend*
- My OCD
- Stress (life's interminable white noise)
- Spaghetti (and other messy foodstuffs)
- Hip Hop (I know I sound ancient now, but – *get a melody!*)
- Marmite (need I say more?)
- Saying things on social media which should only be muttered to yourself when you're stuck in traffic
- The notion that the Bible is just a period book with beautiful language
- Boring expressions of Christianity

On that last point... years ago I heard the actor and director Steven Berkoff talking about a play he was staging, and how people had grown to expect certain things from the theatre. They expected, he said, to doze off part way through. But he was challenging that. He wanted to change expectations. It made me think of church, and expressions of faith where folks just get what they expect, and doze off. I wanted to change that, to express the good news of Jesus in surprising, arresting and unexpected ways.

But back to 101, I would then put the nominations to the vote, so they only go into Room 101 if you agree. So who knows? Spaghetti and Hip Hop may be here to stay. (Yikes!) Not the overused *Legend* though. It's a dead compliment. I mean, come on! It's something that's old and untrue!! What's the point of that??

But to balance things up a bit, how about good things you'd like to bottle so you can give them to anyone who is struggling on a bad day?

Good Things About Life I'd Like to Bottle

- The view from Lee Abbey in North Devon
- Happy songs (pick your own)
- Various movies –
  That Thing You Do
  Raiders of the Lost Ark
  Sing Street
  Notting Hill
  Grease (I'll stop there, I could go on…)
- Adrian Plass's *Sacred Diary*
- That first burst of sunshine in the spring
- Kindness and generosity
- The moment Andy Murray won Wimbledon (Lucy was only four days old, I'd had to wait 50 years!)
- *Have I Got News For You*
- Dancing to *Shotgun* by George Ezra, with Lucy

How about you?

LA Takedown

Once a year the warden took the rest of the leadership away for a two-day retreat, leaving myself and Keith, a pastoral helper, in charge. What could possibly go wrong? Keith and I have become great friends and with each passing year the plots for the Lee Abbey takeover were a time of great comfort and joy.

Things We Did to Lee Abbey While the Leadership Were Away

- Filled the warden's office with stuffed toys
- Placed a welcome sign announcing the place was now a nudist colony (please take a badge and pin it on)
- Chalked a body on the warden's carpet
- Fired all the leadership, handing out their P45s
- Sold the place on eBay
- Burnt it down
- Had an alien invasion
- We all disappeared in the rapture
- Had a nuclear explosion
- Turned the place into a madhouse

- Transformed it into a laboratory for secret government testing

Blokes!

As a result of writing *The Bloke's Bible* I got invited to a fistful of men's breakfasts, teaching days and pub nights. And I learned something. I'm not a proper bloke. The more I went along to these events the more confused I became. At first, when I was still frustrated and angry with church it was fine because I was able to bluster through with my new take on life and faith. But the truth is that I'm not really into sport, DIY, competition or cars. So I often felt intimidated. I'm sure I'm not alone in that. But it's not easy to say this out loud without appearing weak or foolish.

Don't get me wrong, I came away from many events feeling as if I'd been able to help the guys, and my message about the nature of church events not scratching our male itches certainly landed plenty of times. Plus I loved retelling the Bible tales with more honesty and a kind of brutal reality. After one workshop at Lee Abbey, that seemed to come unstuck a bit, I had a letter from a guy about how much it had hit the spot for him. So you can't always tell what is helpful for people.

I think the upshot of all of this is to say that I am a certain kind of artist and as such do not fit the manly image of some these events. (Although, in these gender bending times what is *manly* anyway?) On the plus side, I seem to be able to revisit and retell bits of the Bible in a way that helps men connect with the Good Book. So I'm a walking contradiction! But then, who isn't!

A Few Interesting Blokey Movies (in my opinion)

- *Machine Gun Preacher*
- *Gladiator*
- *The Company Men*
- *About Schmidt*
- *In Bruges*
- *Calvary*
- *Withnail and I*
- *Shawshank Redemption*
- *Groundhog Day*
- *Regarding Henry*
- *Dead Poets Society*

When we first returned to Lee Abbey *Gladiator* was only a couple of years old and lots of the guys I met there really loved it. It set me wondering whether there was a way to make use of that, to draw on their passion for stories like that. *Machine Gun Preacher* is based on the unusual true story of Sam Childers, who rescues families from terrorists in Sudan. It's an action film with radical faith at its heart. I wrote a ten part Bible study course on it, drawing on scenes from the film. *In Bruges* is a dark, shocking film about two hitmen hiding out (guess where?) in Bruges. A group of us guys working at Lee Abbey got together to watch it. Afterwards we stayed and chatted together about so many things.

Shared Language

In 2007 Lynn fell pregnant again. Eleven weeks into the pregnancy she lost the baby. It was a hard 48 hours. Lynn stayed in the hospital overnight, and when I went in to collect her the next day we were both at a very low ebb. One of the nurses could see we were very broken by it all so she came over and said, 'You know, God is with you in this.' We didn't know her at all and don't know if she knew we were Christians. All we know is that right there in that hard place, she was the face and voice of God to us. She was the one who was able to remind us of God present in the suffering. It meant so much.

It's a story I have shared a lot since, and of course, when you talk about trouble and weakness, as hard as this sometimes is, you often discover you are not alone. Many people go through similar experiences. I've come to believe that weakness is a shared language. One we can all speak. Yes, we have our triumphs and joys and celebrations, but we all have our dark times. We often don't realise what problems others have faced until we have a moment to share our own. And the extraordinary thing about Christianity is that our God is right there in the darkness. Understanding our pain. It's both heartening and challenging when Paul tells us, 'Sometimes God's power works best in our weakness.' It's in 2 Corinthians 12 v 9.

Emergency Sex (and other books that inspired me)

We stayed at Lee Abbey for nine years. I continued writing shows, leading houseparties and creating ideas and resources. The drinking subsided slowly. Inch by inch. The whisky first. It was a long road, but when we left and moved into the nearby village of Lynton I developed a version of asthma. It's called cough-variant. This is what finally knocked the drinking on the head. Alcohol makes me cough now. I just don't enjoy it. I was fortunate though, I'd only ever been habitual – pouring drinks regularly after work. So these days I can still have a beer or the like if I choose. But as I say, along with cow's milk and laughter (yes, really!) alcohol often sets me off coughing. Ho hum.

And as the Lee Abbey years went by things were improving. I was in a much better place. I still felt inadequate at times, still wondered what I was doing, still felt a certain kind of malaise, but I'd also found a way forward, and discovered a whole new take on my relationship with God. Someone once told me that when you've been through a desert you always have sand in your pockets, and that's what I believe. The sand of the wilderness is part of what we share. It's the true grit that can help us.

I'd read a ton of helpful books too. Before returning to Lee Abbey in 2002 I had all but given up Christian books. Now a whole load of new authors had come through. Rob Bell, Shane Claiborne, Don Miller, Nick Baines, Nick Page, Tom Wright. I had harboured a secret desire to be able to read the Bible as if I'd never come across it before. These guys were helping me do just that. In a nutshell, I discovered that following Jesus wasn't merely about getting to heaven when we die, and in the meantime biding our time down here. So much is about here. *Your kingdom come on earth as in heaven.* Jesus's parables, his tales of the unexpected, are all about life on earth. How we should follow him through the grit and the grime.

Books That Helped Reawaken my Faith

Praying the Movies – Edward McNulty
Disappointment with God – Phillip Yancey
Messy Spirituality – Mike Yaconelli
Blue Like Jazz – Donald Miller
The Scandal of Grace – Nick Baines
The Irresistible Revolution – Shane Claiborne
Velvet Elvis – Rob Bell
The *New Testament For Everyone* series – Tom Wright
The Wrong Messiah – Nick Page

There are probably others. I do remember coming across a great read called *Emergency Sex* – not a Christian book (there's a surprise) – it was about three UN workers who went to various dangerous countries to make a difference. I also loved *The Year of Living Biblically* by AJ Jacobs about a guy trying to follow the rules of the Old Testament, including checking his clothes for mixed fibres, and not touching anything his wife had touched while she was having her period. She was not impressed.

Over the years I have also been helped and inspired by the writings of Adrian Plass, I first read his *Sacred Diary* whilst at Lee Abbey in 1987. I couldn't believe you were allowed to joke about Christian things in the way he did, but found his honesty and humour so heartening. I frequently revisit his first book, *The Growing Up Pains*, especially when I feel life is falling apart again.

I also love the character of Alan Partridge, both in the TV programmes and the two books he has written. I have laughed so much at his blundering shenanigans. He is the man I fear I may turn out to be! He's of course played by Steve Coogan, who made the film *Philomena*. Now that's a great tale.

Most recently I have been inspired by one of Stewart Lee's book. Lee is an *alternative* alternative comedian, basically he refuses to fall into any known category of comedy. I find him inspiring because he will take an idea, a message if you like, and then completely subvert it and distort it in order to get an audience thinking. He's not a joker for everyone by any means, and some of his stuff passes me by, but I find anyone who is pushing the boundaries of communication interesting.

Nudges

One of the last speakers I heard at Lee Abbey was a guy called Paul Bradbury, who spoke on Abraham. Or Abram as he was at the start of his story. I was fascinated to hear that the first mention of Abe refers to Sarai, his wife. We're told she can't have children. So the inference is that if Abe and his family stay where they are they will fade away, because in his worldview the way to live forever is to have descendants. But if Abe steps out in faith, the promise is that he will be fruitful. That nugget struck a cord with me. It seemed that God might be nudging us out of the nest again, promising fruitfulness beyond the confines of Lee Abbey.

Around this time John Perry, the warden from my time at Lee Abbey in the '80s, came to speak. He told me he'd like to interview me one evening so the guests could hear about what Lynn and I were going to do next. I said I wasn't sure if it would be interesting for the guests but he was adamant. We were doing it! So we sat upfront in the octagonal lounge together and chatted about the future, and I showed some visuals and talked about my desire to share faith in lots of relevant and contemporary ways. And something extraordinary happened. John asked those there that evening if they would consider supporting us. So many of the folk there that night were generous. We were given a heartfelt financial foundation as we set out.

There were other nudges and encouragements, too. I went to speak at a men's event in Exeter, and as I was setting up I noticed a guy sitting on the edge of the stage. We got chatting and he told me how he had given up his job to lead a church. With no steady income. I had never had a conversation quite like this before, and yet it was happening just at a time when we were wondering if we could step out and make a living with me writing and speaking. It was one of those moments where it seemed as if God were there, elbowing me, saying, 'See? See?' I often think timing is everything with miracles like this. We had the question and Mark, the guy on the stage, brought an answer.

By the time we left Lee Abbey David and Pixie Rowe were leading the community. (Lynn and I worked out that we had experienced life at Lee Abbey under five wardens and two acting wardens. We weren't expecting an award of course. Just a big cash prize maybe?) David was keen to see me succeed in the wider world and was a big encourager of my speaking. To that end he offered me a regular mid-week *Film and Faith* workshop spot for the guests at Lee Abbey, while the community held their weekly meeting. It continues to this day, and I'm so grateful to still be a part of Lee Abbey's life and ministry.

Lucy

So in 2011 we left, and moved into a house owned by Lee Abbey for the first six months, while we worked out what to do next. We prayed about the next step and half-expected a door to fall wide-open. Nothing happened. Then, not long before we were due to leave the Lee Abbey house I bumped into a couple of ladies chatting in the street in the village. I knew one of them, Renee, and she introduced me to her friend Kath. We chatted for a while and then I went home. A little later there was a knock at the door. It was Kath. She and her husband Russ owned the house next door to theirs, just across from where we were living. They had been trying to sell the second house but now wondered whether God might be telling them to offer it to us to rent. Boom! The next step.

At Lee Abbey, not long before our leaving, a guest had given me an encouraging message that she sensed was from God for us. 'God will make a way for you,' she told me.
It was happening.

Then in 2012 something else amazing happened. Lynn told me she thought she was pregnant again. Months before we had shared a sad embrace as Lynn told me she was getting rid of all the stuff she'd been keeping in case we had a second child. Now here she was... pregnant. Lucy was born in

July 2013. I had turned 50 the previous December. I often say we're an embodiment of the Bible verse in Proverbs, *you can make your plans, but God has the last word*.

And when I think on the Abram and Sarai story I can't help but smile. I had thought it was about the work we would do. And it certainly was and continues to be, but I hadn't realised that like Abram we would go into the unknown and have a beautiful new baby.

Singing Frog

Back in 2011 a friend messaged me about a story writing competition she thought I should enter. Those brilliant *Divine Chocolate* people were offering a box full of books and ethical chocolate for the best 100-word story. I put her message to one side and forgot about it. Until the date loomed and then I got an idea for a tale about an underwater singing frog, so I rattled it off and sent it in. I won! Yes! Really! Me! I won! I don't tend to win competitions, mostly because I don't enter them, but I won this one. I got a message back telling me the box of goodies would soon be on on its way to me. Excellent.

Just one tiny, teeny, miniscule problem. The competition had been for anyone 12 and under. And no way could I pass, at a weary 48, for that tender age. Even in a darkened room with a bag on my head. I came clean. Told them I had not read the small print, though I did have a daughter Amy who was the great age of nine. They said I could win anyway, mostly with Amy in mind I think. Yay!

If it is of interest, here is my my prize-winning story. (Sorry for any bragging here.) Rereading it now, all these years later, I'm guessing they gave us a scenario about needing to rescue some chocolate stolen by the Chocolate Taker. We pick up the story from there...

The Chocolate Taker

I ran to my secret hideout, hidden at the back of our food cupboard. I walked in, squeezed a bottle of honey, stepped on a packet of biscuits, stuck my finger in a jar of jam, and sat on a bag of marshmallows. This opened a secret shoot in the back wall. I jumped down the tube, straight into the sea in time to see the Chocolate Taker diving in. I swam after him, then pulled out Simon my singing frog and distracted him with it. Then I grabbed all the sweets, swam away and went back to my party.

+ + +

I reckon stories and anecdotes are vital. They give us room to manoeuvre, to see ourselves in the characters and scenarios. They open our minds, stir our hearts and feed our imaginations. And we love them. We pass them on. Whether it's a film, a book, a show, a joke, a bumbling autobiography even?? My hope for this book is it might in some way help you reflect on your own journey so far. A couple of years ago someone told me they preferred the word *safari*. Perhaps journey is a cliché now. So how's your safari been so far?

Much of the biblical wisdom comes to us through stories. Either accounts of lives lived, or tales told by Jesus and others. And these stories aren't safe or easily explained. One day they mean one thing, the next another. They challenge us to think twice, to reassess, to break out. They grab us and shake us when we need waking up, and then at other times they embrace us, warm us and urge us to not give up.

I used to daydream of being famous (who doesn't!!!) practising my awards acceptance speeches. But nowadays I'm inclined to disagree with my younger self. I mean, who'd want to be famous with social media as it is? I'd never cope. Reality is hard enough as it is without trial by smartphone. I'm too fragile, too cautious. So probably best for me to stay famous in my imagination, life's kinder there.

My imagination is where most of my adventuring and derring-do take place anyway. And it's where ideas grow and develop of course. I often find that a daft idea, seemingly too wacky at first, takes hold and develops into something useful and usable. I'm often trying to push ideas, playing with unusual ways of communicating. Drawing sometimes on ideas and stories that don't seem too safe, conventional or spiritual. So if you live in your head as much as in the real world, it can be useful, and you're not alone. There are a good number of us out there. We've been wired up that way.

Boils!

There were many times when I wondered if I would ever manage to be a writer. I desperately wanted to write books but the gap between the kind of writing I could do and the kind of writing that proper authors did seemed to be immense and uncrossable. So many pages need to fill a book! And so many words to fill those pages! And so many letters to fill those words! Undeterred I kept writing over the years, and am actually saddened that I threw much of it away. I only have a few of the stories I put together in my childhood and teenage years. It wasn't great material, but ideas are always precious. Keep everything, you never know when it might prove useful and reworkable in the future. Thank goodness Job didn't throw away his first attempt – *Big Boils on my Bottom*. And that John kept his first apocalyptic scribblings – *Goodness Gracious, Great Bowls of Fire!* (*And darkness, plague, sores, drought and blood!*) A catchy and appealing title.

I had continued writing books for Authentic Media whilst as Lee Abbey, a sequel to *The Bloke's Bible*, a contemporary version of the gospel – *Sons of Thunder*, and a novel based on three Old Testament characters – *No More Heroes*. These were all written with guys in mind, but I didn't realise they weren't selling. I went on happily churning them out. In the end Authentic and I came to a fork in the forest and I took the road less travelled. ☺ The one where you're a writer with no publisher. I'd not imagined this could happen. I thought once you found a publisher you were made for life, to have one and lose one… well! That was something else.

I continued writing, suggesting ideas to Authentic, they were always interested. But nothing came of it. I wrote an entire book which came to nothing – *Long Walk Home*, a rather bleak dystopian novel based on the prodigal son's homeward journey. A lot happens and it's a meandering affair, including a hefty dose of action and adventuring. One day I may tidy it up and put it out there. That's the thing with writing, you tend to live with a hundred and one part-finished projects.

A friend suggested I send a copy of *The Bloke's Bible* to Prince Edward, I had met him at Lee Abbey when he came on a royal visit. I bet he felt astronomically chuffed to have met me. ☺ *!* ('Dave who?') But I'm glad I sent the book and got this appreciative reply.

Dear Mr Haywood,

Thank you so much for your letter of 11th June to The Earl of Wessex enclosing a copy of Bloke's Bible. His Royal Highness has asked me to thank you and say that he looks forward to reading it with pleasure.

The Earl and Countess of Wessex send you and the community at Lee Abbey their best wishes.

Yours sincerely,

Open Door

Sometimes God speaks in a quiet, unassuming way. Just a comment dropped in here or there through someone, nothing dramatic and yet it turns out to change things for good. Back in 2011 when we left Lee Abbey and set out on the next part of this odyssey (by that I don't mean killing mystical creatures or escaping cannibalistic tribes) taking a step towards my being a writer and speaker, a friend Cliff messaged me to say that he hoped I'd make use of Createspace. I'd never heard of that but soon discovered it was Amazon's free-to-use paperback publishing wing. As I mentioned I had by then lost my publisher, and now suddenly – boom! – here was an open door to start writing and publishing again. Createspace has now turned into KDP – but it's still the same tool for publishing paperbacks and e-books. And it's why you are holding this book in your hand now.

In the dark days of 2003 Lynn bought me a copy of Nick Hornby's book *31 Songs.* In it Mr H writes about the songs he loves (yes, there's 31 of them) and tells why he likes them. I loved it. I didn't know a lot of the songs, but it's the kind of book that makes you not care about that. His passion is infectious. So for a while I wondered about writing my own version – *31 Psalms* – unpacking some of the biblical songs and drawing on tunes that I loved.

Free from the daily workload at Lee Abbey I now had time to develop the idea. It became *Rebel Yell* and it was one of the first books I published through Createspace. I also put out *The Dangerous Book for Blokes*. It began life as a third *Bloke's Bible* but had not really worked, so I tweaked it now, and turned it into a different kind of book. I felt that the Bible is a fairly dangerous book when you consider how radically it can change lives. Later I changed the title again to *Pulp Gospel*, can't recall exactly why now, other than I thought it sounded suitably different and unpredictable, and it referenced Quentin Tarantino's film *Pulp Fiction.*

I won't go into great detail about all my writing since 2011, you can find out more on my website. Just to say the next two books I did had also come out of my time at Lee Abbey. I had wittered on for ages about how we needed fresh versions of Jesus's parables, to help us understand something of the challenge and humour of those kingdom tales, I wasn't looking to improve on them, just retell them with my own comments. So *Top Stories* became that book.

I wrote the first draft of *Film and Faith* in 2004. It was a bit of a mountain, because I described and unpacked 66 clips from 66 films, but that meant finding those clips and detailing exactly where they were in the film in case the reader wanted to use the clip in a group setting. I got some A4 copies made and sold them while I was at Lee Abbey. Now here I was able to turn the book into a proper paperback.

In between the writing I started to go out speaking, but the invitations were more scattered than I expected. In fact it's never quite turned out as I imagined. When I was considering this lifestyle a friend and I had drawn up a list of all the possible opportunities – for example a theatre company were interested in putting *The Bloke's Bible* on stage; at that point Authentic Media were interested in my proposal for doing the book on parables. Nothing came of that list, none of it worked out. But other things did, and if you had told me a year before that I would have been able to put out a fistful of books in such a short space of time, I wouldn't have believed it. It wouldn't have seemed possible. My books don't sell like hot cakes, some hardly sell at all, but others have proved to be helpful to people.

I wondered at first how we would survive, not getting lots of bookings or bestsellers. I'd had a certain view of how things should go and those plans were drifting out to sea. Of course God had other ideas, and through the generosity of others has provided so much. Later I read *God's Smuggler* for the first time and reflected on Brother Andrew and his ministry of distributing Bibles. Something of that led me to the conclusion that if I saw what I did as a business then I was failing, but if I saw it as a ministry it was a very different story.

Predictive Preschmictive

Pedantic tents are a pong, aren't they?

Sorry, I mean predictive texts are a pain, aren't they? But they do have the added value of sometimes being hilarious. When my wife and I attended a parents evening at our older daughter's school, Lynn started to feel quite ill, so I messaged some friends to ask them to pray. When I sent a second text I told them that hopefully things would improve soon as she had taken some painkillers. Or rather, what I actually sent was, *hopefully things would get better now because she'd taken some passionkillers.* You couldn't make it up could you. Your phone could, but you couldn't.

One of the big advantages of being a writer now is that there are so many ways you can publish your stuff, and so many styles of writing. Anything goes really. It's... forgive the pun... an open book. You can be an author without ever writing an old fashioned paperback. Some successful books are little more than collections of texts and emails. (That said, there's nothing so new in this. A while back I came across a book called *Address Unknown*. It's a brilliant short novel comprised of letters between two friends, one in America the other in Germany. It was written in 1938 by Kathrine Kressmann Taylor and uses the medium of letter writing in a really smart and subversive way.)

The Bible uses a whole library of styles. And this drives me on, pushes me to experiment, sail close to the wind and be as interesting as I can. To nick ideas from unexpected sources, subvert popular stories, and embrace and redeem the kind of things that we're supposed to be offended by. Jesus's parables are powerful, funny and entertaining. They draw on the life, culture, history and news of his day. He often took well-known yarns and events and gave them an unexpected twist. They are multi-layered tales that will never stop smacking us between the eyes.

Advancements in technology have made such a difference to the way we can work. Before leaving Lee Abbey a guest dropped in a comment about being open to all kinds of opportunities as a writer. So in the last nine years I have continued writing books but also tried to develop other ways of using my communication skills. Social media and the worldwideinterwebnet have opened up a whole feast of possibilities.

I can now publish material online every day of the week. Years ago I heard about the way old Charlie Dickens used to get out and read his stuff to folks at large, and I thought what a great idea. Wouldn't it be good if there was a way to get my stuff out there, freely available, to a wider audience. And that's obviously why they went to all that trouble of inventing Twitter and Facebook. Just for me! So I can share stuff in that way. How kind of them!

This also means I can send resources, readings and drama material to people via email. Lately Simeon Wood and I have recorded two music and narrative reflections and put them on YouTube. Podcasting is all the rage and I occasionally make use of that. I reckon Paul would have loved all this stuff. His letter to the Romans might have well been a blog or a podcast. He might have broken down 1 Corinthians into 400 tweets. (That's just an estimate on the number of verses in the letter. Don't quote me on it.)

Nick Page points out that when Christians started copying and passing round Paul's letters, they did it in codices, little handstitched notebooks, more usually used by tradespeople. They were the new media of the day, not very sophisticated, and the first Christians went – 'Brilliant! Let's make use of that!'

As One Door Closes

The miracles have continued for us as far as house provision goes. In 2014, when we were looking to move from Lynton, we agreed to rent a property in Bideford that would have been much more expensive. But the door suddenly closed on this, and the money we'd given to the estate agent was refunded.

Then Lynn had a dream in which she sensed God was saying that he was the one to go to, as he owned all the properties in the world. So we prayed and soon after heard from Lynn's sister that she was keen to help us buy somewhere. The house next door to some really good friends was on the market. And now here we are in it.

That experience of the door shutting on the other house was a big encouragement really, a reminder that God can close doors to guide us as well as open them. Those words given to us at Lee Abbey continue to ring true. 'God will make a way for you.' We're so grateful for that.

50/50
(N.B. nothing to do with a million-winning lifeline)

One Sunday morning when I had chosen to skip church I was scooting through various books on the Amazon website when I came across something called Flash Fiction. Really short stories. And a book with a title something like 75x75. It featured 75 stories each 75 words long. And my brain started waking up. I loved the idea of very short stories. Quick and easy to read. Maybe I could write a book of short stories. I toyed with the idea for a while and then another idea stuck its head above the wall. What about a thought-for-the-day idea? 50 shorts in 50 words all based on Bible verses. Years ago I had wondered about the idea of doing a collection of creative daily Bible study notes. That of course had come to nothing, but now it re-emerged in this guise.

And so I started posting up daily 50-word readings on Facebook and Twitter. After 50 days I started a new series. That was back in the late summer of 2012. Since then I have used haikus, limericks, TV titles, movies, pop songs, adverts, children's programmes... drawing on all of these and more to create short tales which hopefully turn Bible verses into helpful snapshots. At one point I zoomed through the gospel of Mark, later I zipped through John. My intention was to help folks connect our daily living with the Good Book, which is why I am always looking for ordinary things as inspiration.

Riff Off

One evening I was watching TV when I came across a programme about guitar riffs. I'm a sucker for any pop documentaries so I was immediately hooked. For an hour various guitar heroes analysed and celebrated what made a great and memorable riff. Explaining how a good riff could drive a song forward. And I started thinking. What about a lyrical riff? A short poetic piece featuring a regularly repeated line drawing on a Bible verse and enlarging the meaning of that verse. And so my Wednesday Riffs began. Posted on my website each week for sharing and using. Over time they have morphed into various bits of prose, some with more repetition than others. Here's one from 2015.

Shelter

Those who live in the shelter of the Most High,

Those who abide in the shadow of the Almighty,

Will say to the LORD, "My refuge and my fortress; my God, in whom I trust."

Those who call for help in times of trouble

Those who seek strength to make it through another day

Will say to the LORD, "My refuge and my fortress; my God, in whom I trust."

Those who wrestle to remain calm and compassionate as the world rages

Those who need courage to stand up for truth

Will say to the LORD, "My refuge and my fortress; my God, in whom I trust."

Those who require fresh purpose when the well has run dry

Those who seek solace from the fast lanes of life

Will say to the LORD, "My refuge and my fortress; my God, in whom I trust."

Those who dig deep to keep changing the situation

Those who need shelter when another storm rages

Will say to the LORD, "My refuge and my fortress; my God, in whom I trust."

dh2015

Berlin to Bogota

A couple of years back I watched a film called *Alone in Berlin*. It was based on the true story of a couple in Germany, in World War II. Having lost their son in the war the father, heartbroken and angry, began to leave postcards around the city, warning people to not trust Hitler. He left hundreds around the place, all carefully produced in disguised handwriting. He would place many of them halfway up sets of steps so folks would make eye contact with them as they walked up. It was a highly illegal but ingenious way of resistance. And I started to wonder if I could leave postcards around. Not cards of warning, but of encouragement. Of faith and hope. Then several months went by. I bounced the idea off an artist friend of mine, and it developed a little further.

Then I read about Paige Hunter, who has saved at least six lives on a bridge in Sunderland, by leaving handwritten notes of encouragement tied to the fence. It's the kind of bridge where people go to kill themselves. So Paige wanted to encourage them to think again. She has saved lives, and been recognised for doing so. And somehow that fed into my postcard idea. Notes of encouragement. A few months later I picked up a book in Waterstones by a comedian called Danny Wallace. It was about rudeness and was called *F*** You Very Much*. But of course what it was really about was the opposite. Kindness. And Mr Wallace told the tale of the mayor of Bogota who changed his city with the power of encouragement. He gave out thousands of thumbs up cards and asked folks to give them to others when they saw them doing something good. This was at a time when the city was falling apart because no one really cared. His approach changed things, and I thought, oooh, I'm gonna nick that idea. And suddenly everything came together. The postcards idea, the encouragement notes and the thumbs up cards. And so I got some little business cards printed that said:

Well done!
Really like what
you did there!

And they featured a small thumbs up in the corner. I started offering them when I spoke, in case folks wanted to take some and encourage friends or strangers with them, not really sure if anyone would take any. And it turns out they may be the most important three lines I've written. Not only do folks take them and hand them out, some actually pinch the idea that I pinched and make their own cards! Honestly, it has been so moving and encouraging to hear the stories people have fed back to me. I actually find it quite hard to give out the cards myself and have only handed out a few, but some people love the chance to do it. Changing the world one smile at a time.

All the Wrong Places

I wanted to tell you about the process of these various ideas, not to blow my own trumpet or brag about how wonderful I am, but to explain how I get inspired by unexpected things. Often things that would not necessarily seem to be specifically Christian. In fact, the more these ideas come from the wrong places the more I get inspired by them.

Back in February 2008 I walked into a pub toilet in Brussels. I took one look at the urinals and ran out to get my camera. Now I don't advise taking a camera into a public toilet. It's generally frowned upon, but in this instance the place was empty, PLUS there was a large photograph of four attractive women spanning the wall above the urinals. Just like this one here. In fact it is this one here. This is the picture I took before fleeing.

If you look closely you'll see the third figure even has a camera. I have to confess it made me laugh.

And I was just grateful that in my guilt-ridden haste I got a snapshot that was in focus. But it proved to be more than just a sneaky digital moment, it has given me a picture I have used time and again. Because it's an unexpected image in an unexpected place, and I have used it to help folks think about the unexpected material in the Bible. The funny, shocking, earthy stuff. Like circumcision.

Think about it. If slicing off your... you know... is a sign and reminder of your relationship with God, when are you going to be reminded? When you bathe, go to the loo, and have sex. Now I know this sounds inappropriate. But it's surely true. And vital.

In these very earthy experiences here is the reminder of the God who made earth and experiences. Dust and grit and sex and bodily functions. We may be embarrassed about some of them, but he is surely not. And let's face it, for some folks a little time spent sitting on the loo can be the one gap in the day away from all the rush and bustle. A time when you can read your Bible. And focus a little on God.

Under the Influence

Most Wednesday evenings I work in Lynton cinema, it has one screen, bags of charm and a world-class team of projectionists and ushers. And I'm one of them. If you've ever seen *Cinema Paradiso* it's like that only set in Devon. And I'm Alfredo. If you've not seen it, I'm the bloke what starts the magic lantern and dims the lights. Most of the films that I write about on my website and refer to in my talks I have seen in Lynton cinema. At the end of an evening I drive back home for an hour, listening to Radio 4 and munching junk food to stay alert. Then one night I got caught.

As I pulled in, to park in a space near our house, another car drove slowly past and two females gave me the kind of look which wasn't reassuring. Oh dear. The next thing I know there is a tap on my window and two out-of-uniform, on-their-way-home cops are asking me to please step out of the vehicle. They looked very serious. Various questions ensued. Drugs and drink were mentioned. Having witnessed my driving first-hand, the two were fairly convinced I'd been smoking something that might well start with 'c' and end with 'annabis'.

It's funny how the presence of a policeman can make you feel jumpy. It can almost panic me into doing something illegal.

I hadn't been smoking anything actually but, I don't know about you, when the cops stop you late at night looking rather certain they are going to use handcuffs, you do start to wonder if you've missed something. Had I been stopped recently, one of them asked, studying my number plate rather closely. I hadn't but again – what did I know? Maybe I had and didn't realise it. She seemed so certain. They called another cop, a male, two in fact, so they could search me and the car. With three police cars in our road I felt it might be getting a little out of hand.

Perhaps it was a quiet night. I wondered what on earth Lynn would think if she looked out of the window and saw the shenanigans in the street. The two women then left, along with one of the guys. So it was just me and one cop, who was fairly easy-going really. He didn't search the car after all, but he did pat me down and said he'd like me to blow into this bag please. Which I did. By now I was so jittery I almost wiped the sweat from my brow when he told me the result was negative. In the end it seems I wasn't on drugs, I'm just a terrible driver.

Which is a longwinded way of explaining why my wife often dubs me Frank Spencer. I accept it as a term of endearment. I often take things too seriously and my clumsiness may well be God's way of upending my po-faced approach to myself. And with that in mind, here's a toilet...

Splash!

One Sunday I went to a local church to lead the morning service. I decided I had just enough time to nip to the loo before we started. So I did just that. (I'll keep the details to a minimum here.) The loo had a chain flush, so I reached up to pull it and as I did so the wooden handle came away in my hand. The loo flushed (thankfully) and so I thought I would just quickly hook the handle back on.

I tried. It fell. Into the toilet bowl. Splash. Right in. So two minutes before I'm due to lead the service I have my hand inside the loo, feeling around for this blinking handle. I bet these things never happen to The Pope. Or maybe they do and he keeps quiet. Anyway I didn't keep quiet, I found the handle, dried it off, hung it up and went and started the service by telling everyone about it. I'm a great believer in the power of bungling. Most people can relate to the spirit of Mr Bean. And these things have a habit of happening when I'm attempting to be spiritual. ☺

Billboards

A couple of years ago I saw a film called *Three Billboards Outside Ebbing Missouri.* A scorching, violent, sweary movie. That gave me an idea. It's about a mother who loses her daughter and is so sure the police don't care that she posts up three messages emblazoned on three crimson billboards outside the town. Not a far cry from Jesus's tale about a widow who is desperate for justice and won't shut up about it until those with the power do something. The three red billboards, towering on that big screen, so impressed me that I started to wonder if I could pinch the idea. So I did. I started concocting creative messages in three segments, and posting them on social media as if they were on

Three Billboards Inside Easter, 2018

Three Billboards Inside Easter, 2018

Three Billboards Inside Easter, 2018

three red billboards. Easter was not far off so I used the device as a daily build up to the season of eggs and resurrection. The three above were for Palm Sunday.

I'm Late, I'm Late...

I have always been a late developer. As mentioned before, my memory re childhood didn't really kick in till I was about six. I was still reading kids' books well into my teens (and even now sometimes). I got hooked on the series *Grange Hill* and subsequently *Tucker's Luck* as I neared my twenties. At 37 I had my teenage rebellion. And give me enough time alone in the kitchen and I'll fish out my old punk tracks and drown the house out. Just recently our six year old Lucy came in to ask me to please turn the music down. A sweet moment of role reversal there methinks. I don't ever recall having to pop into the kitchen to ask dad if he could play Frank Sinatra just a little more quietly. I got married at 31, became a father at 39, then again at 50.

Nothing of this is unusual these days though. I'm heartened by how many folks now become parents later on in life. But it all fits rather nicely with my refusal to properly grow up. I have often felt adrift at dinner parties and events full of sensible adults. They are probably not sensible at all of course, they've learned over the years how to behave properly. And I haven't. As I plough on through my 50s I'm grateful for the ability to still think, and occasionally act, like a 20 year old. I'm hopelessly out of touch with YA (Young Adult) culture of course, and much of it doesn't appeal, but there are still some bits that seep into my consciousness. Not least when I am speaking in public.

One of my favourite clips at the moment is a version of the hymn Amazing Grace sung by the Irish punk band the *Dropkick Murphys.* It's always quite fun to ask if there are any fans in the audience or congregation when I show it, knowing full well that most folks will not have heard of the DKMs. That said I did recently meet someone who had been to one of their concerts just a few weeks before. So there you go – you never know!

This refusal to grow up has come in rather useful in my work. Back in my 20s and 30s I was quite happy to slap on a white face and go out in public doing the kind of drama which hopefully made all the grown-ups stop in their tracks and reassess just a little. They might well of course have thought I was just being an idiot. But then the sensible folks thought that about Jesus too. Nowadays when I lead church events one of my main aims is to avoid being boring. I have been bored in church all my life, and I'm a great believer in the power of entertainment for communicating truth. So I do my best to offer the unexpected. To surprise, humour and shock. Not for its own sake, but to help folk experience and remember. I don't want people to come away having just been to a talk, I want them to experience something.

Killjoy

I'm a killjoy really. I am when it comes to Disney anyway. Their animations have never really toasted my marshmallows. And in recent years I have realised that often their movie message is – *just believe in yourself and you can do anything*. Yea right. You see, as far as I'm aware, when God appeared to Moses in a burning bush he didn't say, 'Oh go on Mo, don't  worry about your past and your fears, just believe in yourself and you'll be able to part the Red Sea.' And when an angel popped in on Mary he didn't say, 'Just believe in yourself and you'll have a baby.' No. I believe the message was about God enabling them. God being with them. God helping them.

A few years back we went to Walt's big playpark in Paris. I braced myself. Admittedly I did have some fun, and my wife and daughter loved it. Then I spotted this opportunity. Walt and the mouse. I figured what we were all really doing was worshipping the Mickey Maestro. So I thought I'd go all prophetic and illustrate that, Ezekiel style. I got down on my knees and began bowing before his Disney-ness. A hush settled over the place. Rides came to a standstill. Children stared, candy floss frozen in mid-air. The staff threw off their Daffy Du… oops sorry… I mean *Donald* Duck costumes. Tumbleweed engulfed the place. In my dreams. In reality? Nobody noticed. No one saw me worshipping the mouse because they were all too busy worshipping the mouse. Ho hum.

You might think I'm overdoing it a bit and well, I guess I am really. But I'm just pointing out that worship is about where we spend our time, money, energy and talents. It's more than the songs we sing and prayers we pray, though they are certainly a big part of it. But ultimately worship is about what we give, what we spend, and where we direct that. So we all have idols really. I love chocolate. I don't fall on bended knee before every cream egg I down, but that's not to say it doesn't hold an important place in my life. I just reckon we need to be honest and that way we can face these worship struggles. Remember the folks who disrupted Micah's afternoon? How can we better worship God? Bigger offerings of corn? they asked. Nope, snapped Micah, who was obviously wanting to get back to watching his favourite team on Channel Prophet. (You get the feeling this happened to him most Saturday afternoons.) It's the way you live, he says. That's how you worship. You can check it out in Micah 6 verse 8.

And that's why all our worship is flawed. Thanks for setting the bar so high Micah. ☺

Perhaps it's just a matter of being honest. We all have divided loyalties. We all get distracted and look for comfort in various things. God knows that. Thank goodness we can keep coming back to him and redressing the balance. Surely that's the point of grace, hope, mercy and forgiveness. What's the difference between Bing Crosby and Walt Disney? Bing sings but Walt disney. (You need a Scottish accent.)

'Is...   this...   the...   way...   out?'

Three Days in 2017

An apology, if the following seems familiar it may well be that you have read it in my book *Turning Tables*, about the God who upends our expectations and ideas. If it doesn't seem familiar, gadzooks! Why haven't you read my book *Turning Tables*, about the God who upends our expectations and ideas? It's a modern classic. In my mind anyway. 😊 But once again dear gentle reader I digress, on with the familiar/unfamiliar chapter…

I have come to love a couple of verses from Song of Songs chapter 2. 'I am my beloved's and my beloved is mine. My dove is hiding behind some rocks, behind an outcrop on the cliff. Let me see you; let me hear your voice. For your voice is pleasant, and your face is lovely.'

I came across these verses while taking some time out to reflect on God, to try and be still. This was back in 2017. Ever tried just being still? Man, it's tricky. A million ideas crowd into your head. Drinking tea, drinking coffee, eating chocolate, walking, listening to music, reading, drumming your fingers, sitting somewhere else other than here, doing stuff, doing other stuff, doing still other stuff. Doing doing doing. I mean, after all, what's to be gained doing nothing? Well, plenty as it happens.

'Let me see you; let me hear your voice.'

As I read these verses from Song of Songs it was as if a switch got flicked inside me. They are so tender, so kind, so encouraging, as if God were beckoning to me, drawing me to come closer – because he likes me. He likes my face and my voice. He wasn't just putting up with me because of everything that Jesus has done for me. He loves me, because he made me, and yes, his Son paid everything for me. And he loves to be with me, he loves to see me and hear me.

It felt like a risk, like crossing a line, to trust those words, yet once I took a step, everything was a little different. And then I watched *Brooklyn*, about Eilis and Tony, two cautious lovers, two people who want to know each other, to love each other, but are shy and nervous about it. And it seemed to capture the moment.

When Eilis finally does reply to Tony's declaration of love she tells him that she likes him, and likes being with him, and perhaps feels the same way. And if he ever tells her again, she will say she loves him too. Tony is sideswiped. He can't believe it, he thought they were going to have a vastly different kind of conversation and can't resist doublechecking with her. 'You really love me?' he asks, amazed and quietly overjoyed.

Back in 1985 I had discovered this kind of divine unconditional love breaking into my life, through a close relationship. Anna was someone who embraced and embodied the love of God in an extraordinary way. She challenged me to trust in that love and open myself to it. I glimpsed for the first time the reality that God loved me and I could love him. It was a profound and radical few months. It may sound odd to have only discovered this several years after becoming a Christian (remember I said the story was messy), but before this I had been focused on getting saved and avoiding hell. The rescuing side of God if you like. Now Anna was showing me another side of God. A liberating lifegiving God, full of kindness, joy and wonder. It was a precious, extraordinary time. It transformed my life for a while. But I let it slip away. Lost sight of it. I became focused on achieving things for God, trying to be successful for him, rather than allowing his love and care to draw things from me.

Now here I was, back at Lee Abbey decades later, discovering it all over again. Having another chance to know the depths and reality of that love. It had never gone away really, I had glimpsed it on and off over the years, but here was a new beginning.

I wonder how much of this is about appreciating the present moment, being here now, and becoming aware of the affirming presence of God with us, on our side. Taking time to tune in.

Cautious

I can be so cautious about trusting this divine love, this kindness, this compassion. I can be reluctant about stepping out from behind my rocks; it's risky, I feel vulnerable without the masks and escape hatches. Without my Eden fig leaves. I've discovered that it's not easy to sit for a moment with God, daring to hold on to those words which promise that he loves our presence, to see our faces and hear our voices.

'Take a long, loving look at God,' Psalm 46 urges us in The Message version. Not merely coming with our shopping list prayers, but talking with him. About anything. The bits of nonsense and the bags of happiness and shedloads of pain. And being silent. Saying nothing. Letting the unsaid be the unsaid. Sometimes we have no words. We only have our chaotic worlds. Our presence. So we try and bring that. Sitting, standing, with nothing to say. Just offering our time. It's liberating and yet so hard to do!

We hide, we play hard to get, we fear rejection, we have been battered in the past. We have had to earn acceptance. We have been ridiculed for being foolishly honest. We know that trust can be misused, vulnerability can lead to trouble. Our precious dreams can be trampled upon, made fun of, discarded. People may well misunderstand and ridicule.

So like Eilis we need to reflect, we need to know this is not pretence. Not a ruse, not a trap to make us look stupid. We long for something good. But it may take us time to poke our heads above the parapet. To stick our noses out from behind our rocks. From our safe, well-padded, well-protected places. So God waits, and does his best to assure us that he loves our faces, and our smiles, and our voices, and our longings, and our dreams. To upend our misconceptions that he is out to trick us or trap us or hurt us; whispering to us, through the nudging of his spirit, the friendship of others, the encouraging verses in his Bible, and perhaps just a little through some of the words in this book. On this page perhaps.

My default setting is always to believe I am not valuable, to think of all those reasons why God would not like me. To think I must 'get it right' so he will grudgingly accept me. Each morning, as I pause and reflect, even for a second, on God's kindness, it's as if that setting gets changed, to God's default option. His compassion. His risk-taking love. His raging grace, which tenderly runs rampant through the obstacles I set up. Down the cluttered corridors of my being. Tipping up all the tables of logic and conditioning along the way.

It's a bit of a battle, I often overthink it, forget that it's his work to do the resetting, his desire, his pleasure. For me it's about letting go, realising again that there's nothing I can do except stand there. And be with him. One translation of Psalm 46 v 10 says, 'Be still and *experience* that I am God.' It's beyond head knowledge, and logic, and calculations, and wheeler-dealing. It's beyond feelings, though I often gently sense his presence. I guess it's a lesson I'll go on learning forever. I'm so keen to rush off and 'do things.' This is only my story. Yours will be different. But I hope it's of some encouragement.

Peace Beyond

The call to waste time, to risk everything on doing nothing,
To step out of life's traffic even for a few seconds.
For a breath here and there, a pause in the pressing flurry,
To celebrate the free gift,
No upgrades required or hidden extras.
Stopping and staring,
Slowing down to take that long, loving look,
Adopting for the briefest of interludes
Those unforced rhythms of grace.
Allowing healing access to the deep waters,
The unknown pools of our being,
The secret places that drive us, stall us, trip us,
Make us react as we do.
There may be silence or not, we may be restless or still,
Choosing to brake for just a moment, making a start,
Easing that calming stick in the spokes of our life.
Not easy, when we want to be kept busy, distracted, fuelled,
When 5 seconds, or 10 or 30 can seem like an age.
Yet the call goes on, to buck the trend,
Stop filling every glimmer of time,
With so much stuff that we're left empty,
Plugging for a moment back into God and all that makes sense,
A peace offered, accessible and beyond our understanding.

Sunshine

Rowan Williams talks of stepping into the sunshine. When we sunbathe we don't have to do anything, if we put ourselves in sunlight we will change a little, pick up even the faintest of tans. So it is with God. When we set aside our time, give him our quiet attention, step into his sunlight, something of him will rub off on us. We worship him with our silence and stillness and it shapes us in some small way.

Now of course it's easy to write of this, still a challenge to do it. Every time I step aside for a minute or two a million other ideas invade my head. It's always a fight to stop and be still. To take a long loving look at God, as The Message says in Psalm 46.

Those two days in 2017 have changed me though, they have changed my view of prayer. And when I wondered how I could pray for others, something again, that I am not good at, an idea crept into my mind. I made a cross from a bit of cardboard and started writing names on it, those I wanted to pray for. After a while I started typing these names in a tiny font, because the cross is small and I was starting to fill it up. This is it.
I now carry this with me in my pocket, and every so often, I slow down and focus on the presence of God, and when I do that I bring all these people with me. That's my prayer.

In Pieces

I was on a Lee Abbey church mission in Wales when a member of the team gave out a box of jigsaw pieces and asked everyone to take one. She then spoke about how we are all an important part of God's picture in the world. All different colours, shapes and sizes. But precious and vital. I loved this and have been using it myself ever since. One Christmas I even wrote a story about it to send out with our cards.

The Jigsaw

A young girl wanted to encourage her class, so she bought a rather expensive jigsaw as a Christmas present and gave it to them on the last day of term. The teacher gave a weary sigh and rolled his eyes as he saw the class's pleading gaze, this disrupted his carefully prepared plans for the last few hours of term. He reluctantly gave in and the class spent the afternoon putting the picture together before going home to celebrate Christmas. Left alone with the picture of a cartoon stable and some vividly-coloured shepherds the young girl wondered what to do with it now. So she took it apart and wrapped up each individual piece. Then she cycled round to the homes of her classmates and pushed one piece through each door. She was on her way home in the fading light when she stopped. An idea had snuck into her head but she was not sure if she should do it. She didn't want to look stupid or get into trouble. Eventually she turned her bike around.

Her teacher came home late that evening, picked up the post on his mat and put it to one side on top of all the other unopened bills and cards. He only found the little packet tucked between the letters, when he fished through the postal mountain on Christmas morning. He opened the tiny parcel, found a bright jigsaw piece, and turned it in his fingers. On the back, in precise, neat handwriting, it said, *You're really great. Thanks for being our teacher.* The teacher cried. Bone-tired from a hard term and some difficult students he had wondered if he was doing anything useful at all. He held the precious piece in his hand, closed his fist around it and pressed it to his chest for a long time. Then he found a silver picture frame, took out the old photo and framed the jigsaw piece inside. At the start of the following term he placed the frame on his desk, and kept it there for the next 30 years. Whenever other staff or pupils asked him about it, he replied, 'It reminds me that I don't always realise the good I'm doing. I'm a vital part of a bigger picture, it keeps me going when I want to give up.'

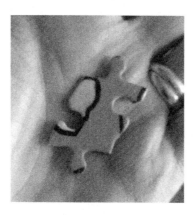

My Little Finger

I have a problem. It began last year. You see, like most people I have two little fingers, the one on my left hand is a fairly fine example of little fingerness. But, the one on my right hand is not. It used to be, but not now. Due to an infection the left side of the nail looks like I keep hitting it with a sledgehammer. Or as if it is badly stained from smoking too many cigarettes. The likelihood is it will remain that way. It began with a swollen joint and now look where it's ended up.

 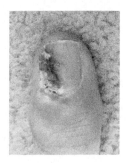

So I take it along with me when I speak. Obviously it would be coming anyway but it's a useful illustration. Remember that prolific letter writer Paul? The one who would have loved social media if he were around now? Well he created a cartoon picture about parts of the body arguing with each other. The eye saying to the hand, sorry I won't be seeing you anymore. The ear saying to the bottom, I've had enough of listening to you. That sort of thing. You can check it out in 1 Corinthians chapter

12. It was about people rather than body parts. People falling out and fracturing the body of Jesus on earth. We're all imperfect aren't we? I mean obviously I *was* perfect till my fingernail started resembling a dead slug. And at any one time some parts of God's body on earth (clue: us) are strong, others are weak. Some are doing well, some are in pain. Some look fine, others like a dead slug. And so it goes on.

The point is that my dodgy finger is still my finger. It still functions. Still plays a vital part in my life. And that's why we need truckloads of patience because we are all going to wind each other up with our various strengths and weaknesses, preferences and personalities.

Just on the weaknesses thing. Adrian Plass talks about bringing our weaknesses to God to see what he might do with them. This is counter-cultural to some Christian teaching which highlights getting sorted out by God before he can use us. Doing *The Bloke's Bible* and a later book *Diary of a Wimpy Christian* were opportunities to offer my weaknesses for God's use. I began the *Wimpy Diary* with Paul's quote about gladly boasting about his weaknesses. I guess it's back to that shared language again. And offering our weaknesses as channels for God's strength. We're all fragile really. I'm so grateful God continues to use us in our shambolic ragged state.

Ambush!

Life ambushes us. I saw this ice cream and couldn't resist taking a picture. It seemed to perfectly sum up the way life ambushes us sometimes. In smaller and larger ways. We make our plans, buy our ice creams and then whoomf. Scuppered.

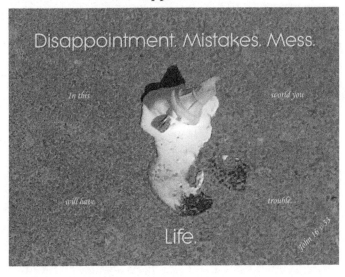

It's the way isn't it?. That's why I included those words from Jesus about having trouble in this world. He warns us about it. That following him won't necessarily make life easier. In fact for many it makes life more difficult, more complicated, even more dangerous. But there's an empty sign above all that, an empty cross. A vacancy where there should be hopelessness and death. Because he has overcome the world and all its pain, trouble and unexpected twists and turns.

Cutting Room Floor

I am not a film critic, not at all. I'm not even sure I'm a movie buff. I think I'm just someone who loves stories and the way one story can remind us of another. Can help us connect to another bigger story. I also think the Bible is hard to read. Must be or the tubes and buses and trains would be crammed with folks reading and re-reading it. And so using films and other stories which are high on entertainment value to help folk connect with the Good Book is something I love. Could be a movie moment, or a TV programme, or an internet joke, or a news story. They are all up for grabs. But I'm not a critic. I know because I watch and read critics and my head just doesn't work in that way. I'm even cautious about recommending films as I've learned that what I like may not be your tub of popcorn at all.

Years before I began drawing on film in the way I do now I would occasionally watch a film and think *if I was a vicar I'd use that scene*. Someone once said I have a mind like a cutting room floor. They may be onto something as I do seem to have a memory for movie moments and individual scenes. They lie around in my head waiting for me to bore my family with repeated descriptions of them or drop into my talks. Sometimes I love scenes rather than the movie itself.

And not only movies. The Hot Chocolate song *It started with a kiss* has long reminded me of Judas and what he began that night in Gethsemane. Deacon Blue's track *Loaded* seems to me to be all about the Rich Fool parable. And when Paul Whitehouse has his 'Brilliant!' character on *The Fast Show* commenting comedically on the Nativity scene, well it's tailor-made for a Christmas sermon surely. Just because these things don't come with a Christian tag doesn't mean they aren't useful devices. None of Jesus's parables mention God. They are all stories drawn from regular life.

My head is a strange land, movies, pop music, chocolate, the Bible, stories, Jesus and stress all seem to rattle around in there vying for supremacy. Along with the usual preoccupations that come with being a human being. I tend to overthink things too. I find going to church quite stressful these days as being with lots of people takes its toll on me. I'm hopeless at small talk so knowing what to say to people is not easy. I guess I have a writer's brain, and with writing you can make several attempts to get a sentence right. In conversation, once you say it the first time, it's out there. You can't rewrite it. I could just write post it notes to people, but then they'd think I was mad.

Posting Signs

I keep various notes to myself on my desktop to help me through. I need encouragement because I often question if I'm doing the right thing. My wife Lynn recently said to me, 'Better to do an imperfect something, than a perfect nothing.' So I have that there. Plus a quote from an email sent to me by a dear friend at a time when I was wondering if I was on the right track. He sent me a message saying he'd been praying for me and felt God was encouraging him to tell me to keep going with what I am doing. Amazing! He could have had no idea about my questions.

I have a quote from one of Pete Greig's books – *God puts salt on our lips to make us thirst for him.* It's something old Saint Augustine once said. I like it and wonder what different kinds of salt God uses for different people. There's a post-it saying - *Dare I be true to myself?* Because often I feel the need to say what I think should be said, rather than what I want to say. There's a barely readable scribble – *subvert secular stories.* I like that one, grabbing what is out there and giving it a twist for God's kingdom.

The message version of Psalm 71 verse 16 says this: 'I come in the power of the Lord God, I post signs marking his right of way.' I love that, and I hope, just maybe, to be part of it, posting signs of all kinds, often drawing on unexpected sources.

Lockdown

I recently read of the author Peter May, who wrote a book 15 years ago called *Lockdown*, about a pandemic. No publisher would touch it, saying it was too unbelievable. Prompted by a friend he dug it out again recently and approached a publisher, who read it overnight and immediately decided to publish it. If someone had told us six months before Covid-19 that the world would be living behind closed doors we couldn't have imagined it. It would have seemed unbelievable. When we think of the Easter events, the mysterious and extraordinary hope of resurrection, and the eternal living presence of Jesus, it's not always easy for us to grasp these things. An understatement perhaps! But, as different as it is, this story of Peter May reminds me that extraordinary things happen. We just can't always grasp what is beyond our present experience and reality.

Who Am I?

A strange question you might think after having just attempted to string together rather a lot of words on the subject. But I have just been listening to a radio programme about the actor Peter Sellers. In it reference was made to something Sellers himself had said, that he had no personality of his own, which may be why he was so good at playing roles.

I've sometimes wondered this of myself, who am I really? I'm not sure if I would go so far as to say I've no personality, but I do often wonder which one is the real me. I fear that I define myself by who I am with. Attempting to be what I think others want me to be. This does refer back a bit to my tendency towards compartmentalising, because I perceive different people to be in different compartments of my life. The downside of all this is that I can feel people are making demands on me that I cannot meet. The upside is that I am able to adjust my public presentations depending on my audience. Changing things so they work best for each scenario even as I'm up the front delivering my thoughts.

I wonder if this is why I find being with others so tiring, because I'm constantly trying to be what I think is required of me. Constantly trying to work out what is expected and to adjust to that, and thus wearing myself out.

The advantage of writing, and I often feel more relaxed when doing this, is that I am not trying to be something else. I'm just being Dave the writer. Even if I am sometimes adjusting what and how I write depending on my audience.

This is why I want to run from social situations. Even happy parties can feel too much like hard work sometimes. It's a shame of course, because friendly gatherings are arranged so people can get together and enjoy each other's company. But sadly it's a struggle for me and for others who are similar. Even eating in public is a challenge for me, give me a crumbly or chewy biscuit and I'll most likely pocket it until the conversation is over.

We often say that God knows us better than we know ourselves. I hold on to that. At least someone understands why I am the way I am. And indeed *who* I really am. I'm a big fan of Psalm 139. A description of the God who sees us in all our various guises. *Whether we sit or stand* in verse 2 I take to mean, wherever we are, whatever we're doing and whoever we are trying to be. The Good News version of Psalm 29 v 10 tells of God ruling over the deep waters – or as I see it, he understands the deep places of our being. What makes us tick if you like.

I think I am most myself when I'm alone with God, and of course Lynn knows me better than any other human, probably better than I realise. Twenty-five years together does tend to do that. You can't help but let yourself leak out during so many days and nights of life's mundane and extraordinary safari.

Lynn is kind and sensitive, smart and funny, gentle and beautiful, and somehow copes with my volatility and madness. She's also patient and courageous and sometimes a bit of a wonderful airhead. But then so am I so we go together well!

Mum and Dad

Sadly mum passed away in May 2010, after being ill for a while. She was in Weston hospice for a couple of days before she died and our family shared a precious time together. Mum wasn't conscious but it was almost as if she and God had made a plan to slow us all down and get us to appreciate being together for a little while. We laughed and cried, talked, played games, did crosswords. We were a family.

My parents had both been into amateur dramatics before we were born and so I guess I get my dramatic streak from them. But my mum too was happy at home and I may well have got my introversion from her. She was a great cook, always serving up the likes of shepherd's pie or meat and potato pie, or liver and onions, fry-ups, homemade cakes, jam tarts, apple pies, tiramisu, curry. And no one served up boiled eggs and soldiers the way she did. Ah... such memories.

And speaking of food – mash potato always reminds me of my mum. Or rather, *mashing* potato. I must have watched mum do it a lot when I was little because there is something so soothing, so fulfilling, so pleasing about doing it now. I'm that dedicated to it I'll leap at the chance if there is a masher and a pan of hot spuds around. Let no one get in my way. There is something satisfying and almost magical about seeing those off-white lumps transform into creamy smooth slopes and hills. It's like a work of art, like creating a delicious masterpiece from steaming raw materials.

Dad on the other hand was a big fan of door-to-door evangelism, and I went along with him sometimes. He was so at ease with it, ringing the bell and waiting to chat to a stranger about his faith. He was never fazed by the challenges. He's the one person I know who loved door knocking. My sister Liz is great at talking to people as well. She loves relating to others and definitely got that gift from my dad.

After mum died dad soldiered on with Liz and Martin's vital help for a couple of years, but he was not well and needed more care, so eventually he moved into a residential care home. We continued spending time with him until he died in June 2018. I find funerals totally overwhelming so wasn't able to share anything publicly at either of my parents' services, but I was able to put some pictures together for a presentation at my dad's funeral. We had shared many happy times together, bantered about many things, and watched many war films and cowboy movies. He loved *The Dambusters, The Great Escape, The Magnificent Seven* and *The Longest Day* as well as classics like *Regarding Henry* and *The Railway Children*. Two films that made us both cry.

Mum and dad had been so supportive of Liz and I through all our ups and downs. They had always believed in us and wanted the best. When I started printing my own drama books we got a comb binding machine and dad did all that side of things for me. When *The Bloke's Bible* came out he read it several times and was so encouraging about it.

When I first scribbled down *Basil the Friendly Ghost* it was mum who typed it up and stapled the pages together to make my first book. When I gave up a good career in banking to go to Lee Abbey in '84 they were right there with me. Supporting me in what I wanted to do. A week before leaving Lee Abbey that first time in '88 I performed my first solo mime gig in the Octagonal lounge there. They were in the audience that night. It was hard for them when things fell apart for Lynn and I in the late '90s but they kept on praying for us. When we moved to Derbyshire and did up the cottage they came and helped. I can see mum now, not so young anymore, sat on a stool scraping old flaking paint off one of the window frames.

They were staying with us in Woking when the first drama book published by Church House arrived. We opened a bottle of champagne to celebrate that thrilling moment. It was a friend of my mum's who told me years ago in Cornwall, 'If you want to be a writer you should read plenty of other people's books, and travel.' I've managed to do a bit of both.

Us in the 60s... and again just a few lifetimes later

Turning

When I was somewhere in the region of 19 or 20 I used to listen to a song by Randy Stonehill called *Turning Thirty*. It was about just that, supposedly sung by Mr Stonehill on the eve of his milestone birthday. That moment seemed so far away to me at that early point in my life. And a lot would certainly happen before I crossed that line. Now here I am only a couple of years away from turning 60. Can't believe it really. I played that song again the other day. It stirs up the old memories, kindles all kinds of feelings.

Time is a strange thing. A few years ago I tried to capture something of my thoughts about it in this short piece.

Tides
Sometimes I feel overwhelmed by the tides of time.
We stand on the beach like a million postmodern Canutes proving yet again that we can't hold back the water.
And never could.
Even when we were strong and young and angry and noble.
We were merely ignorant of the nature of that sea.
Second by second it has continued washing in and out.
The water keeps moving, the one who made it keeps calling, and we cannot stand still.

The Last Crusade

Thanks for ploughing through these strange recollections and reflections. I'll leave you with one of my *Film Friday* thoughts, from one of my all-time favourite movie characters.

Indiana Jones and his dad are out there searching for the Holy Grail, the cup used at the last supper. On reaching the caves where this is hidden Indy discovers that he must pass three tests to get to the cup and save his father – tests about humility, the name of God and steps of faith. The last test involves crossing a ravine with no obvious bridge. It's only as he takes a step that the way across becomes clear.

Humility, God and faith. In this case they are three tests, in life itself, we might call them crucial priorities. Following Jesus has always been a strange mixture of hope and challenge. Comfort and discovery. Steps of reassurance and steps into the unknown. 'Step out of the traffic, take a good long look at me, discover the unforced rhythms of grace. Take up my approach and my ways of living, for they are good. My burdens are light.' But he also says, 'Take up your cross and follow me.' Both and. One with the other. Hope and challenge. Compassion and justice. Truth and love. There is a lovely verse in Psalm 85 which sums this up.

'Wisdom and mercy have embraced. Unfailing love and truth have met together. Righteousness and peace have kissed!'

Jesus brings together these aspects of full life. 'Truth springs up from the earth, and righteousness smiles down from heaven.' Psalm 85 goes on. A cross rises from the dust, fulfilling the promise of new life, on earth as in heaven.

Indy is on his way to finding life and healing for his father, but it involves stepping across a valley. Keeping going though the way is uncertain. Though he is afraid and learning as he goes. We face these kinds of valleys ourselves and need help to keep walking. We need wisdom and mercy, love and truth to help us. Winston Churchill famously said, 'When you're going through hell... keep going.'

Lord, please help us, today, tomorrow, and the day after, to do just that, to keep going, with you, Amen.

I don't have it all figured out

I love life but it scares me
I believe in hope but sometimes despair
I believe in caring but sometimes folk bug me
Some days I like them some days I don't
Sometimes I think I'm winning
Sometimes I feel as if I'm losing

Because I don't have it all figured out yet

I want to smile but often scowl
I long to be upbeat but find myself complaining
Want to be understanding but frequently judge
I want to help but often hinder
Some days I seem to have all the answers
Some days I don't have any at all

Because I don't have it all figured out yet

I know what I think and then I don't
I have my principles then lose them
I want to fight for truth and justice
Then I want to throw in the towel
I know where I'm heading then
Feel suddenly lost all over again ...

Because I don't have it all figured out yet

DAVE HOPWOOD 2020

**Poster by Sarah Prentice Design & Illustration
With thanks too to Clare Jefferis for the concept**

Printed in Great Britain
by Amazon

64693099R00132